Grandparenting a Child with Autism

The Joy, Frustration, and Growth of Living with Autism

SYLVIA MILLER GRUBB
with *Stuart E. Grubb*

To my good friend, Jan — and fellow bibliophile —

Sylvia

Quill House Publishers
Minneapolis, Minnesota

Grandparenting a Child with Autism
The Joy, Frustration, and Growth of Living with Autism
by Sylvia Miller Grubb with Stuart E. Grubb

Copyright 2012 Sylvia Miller Grubb. All rights reserved. No part of this book may be reproduced or transmitted in any form by any means, electronic, mechanical, recording, or otherwise, without the express permission of the publisher. For information or permission for reprints or excerpts, please contact the publisher.

Neither the publisher nor the author warrant or assume any legal liability or responsibility for the accuracy, completeness, or usefulness of any information presented in this book.

ISBN 13: 978-1-933-79450-X
ISBN 10: 1-933794-50-1

Library of Congress Control Number: 2011944992

Quill House Publishers, PO Box 390759, Minneapolis, MN 55439
Manufactured in the United States of America

Dedicated to the memory of my brother, Duane Miller.

Duane showed us how to enjoy life.
Physical limitations were no barrier.

Contents

PROLOGUE
An Odyssey 9

INTRODUCTION
Setting the Scene 11

DIAGNOSIS
The Journey Begins..17

SENSORY ISSUES
A Christmas Party 27

LANGUAGE CHALLENGES
"I Couldn't Have Done It Without You"......................34

INTERPERSONAL RELATIONSHIPS
Micah Shares Valentines 37

COMMUNICATION
Taylor Emails Micah..42

PUBLIC PARTICIPATION
A Musical Turn Around 53

CELEBRATIONS AND EVENTS
The Birthday Party 59

ALLERGIES, IMMUNIZATIONS, AND SPECIAL DIETS
Micah Is Sick Again 66

FOOD FAVORITES AND AVERSIONS
Micah Tries Krabby Patties..72

THERAPEUTIC ACTIVITIES
Micah Meets Sam 80

DEVELOPING NEW INTERESTS
Micah's Favorite Sport—Swimming 87

SIBLING RELATIONSHIPS
Micah as a Brother 94

RELATIONSHIPS IN THE EXTENDED FAMILY
We Visit Micah's Cousins in Kansas City 99

COMMUNITY RELATIONSHIPS
Micah's Family Builds a Team 103

TRAVEL EXPERIENCES
We Go to Washington, D.C. 109

RELIGIOUS TRADITIONS AND TRAINING
Micah Is Confirmed 116

PREPARING FOR EMPLOYMENT
Micah Gets a Job 124

FINANCIAL FUTURE
Setting Up a Special Needs Trust 135

A Closing Thought 136

To Micah from Grandpa 137

Acknowledgments 138

Bibliography 139

Autism is a developmental disorder
that appears in the first three years of life,
and affects the brain's normal development
of social and communication skills.
People with autism have symptoms or difficulty
in three areas:
social interaction, language as used for social interaction,
and repetitive interests or behaviors.
Today it is estimated that one in every 110 children
is diagnosed with autism.

Autism Society of America, 2011

Micah's family: Muriel, Susan, Micah, and Stuart

PROLOGUE

An Odyssey

Grandparenting a child with autism can be like standing on the bank of a rushing river watching a dramatic and traumatic scene unfold before you. Your grandchild, your child, and your child's family are in a small boat on that river, trying mightily to stay afloat. You want to help them, but it is difficult to know how.

When your child's family started this adventure, everyone had expectations of what was downstream. The boat was packed with provisions and supplies they would need along the way. There would be unexpected twists, turns, and snags, but they were ready to deal with them. The river would not always be smooth. It would require a lot of strength and hard work to complete the journey. At least there were channel markers and helpful people to guide the way and keep the family on track. And when the family did get to the end of the river, they would look back on the journey and challenges with fond memories. When the child was born, they pushed off from the bank and started downstream.

In the first years, the journey was going according to plan. Your grandchild was generally healthy. His parents were overworked and tired, but that was to be expected. They had been paddling hard and making decisions that would keep the boat above water, navigating away from rocks and shallows, and pushing the boat back to open water when it got stuck.

At some point the river split into two channels. The current carried the boat into one of the channels, as it had numerous times before. There was no reason to be concerned. All channels eventually lead to the same place, right? But gradually things began to look troubling.

Your grandchild was not talking like he used to. He was not playing with the other kids at day care and sometimes did not even look at adults. He was starting to make odd motions with his hands.

Your grandchild's parents noticed changes also, and eventually began to paddle furiously against the current that was pulling their family toward some unknown danger. They may have kept quiet, preferring to deal with the situation themselves, or they may have been yelling for anyone's help. Maybe there was a doctor who could offer a safe landing site? Maybe at least someone could tell them what was around the river bend, so they could know how to prepare and brace themselves?

Getting a diagnosis of autism can be like going over a waterfall. The child, the boat, and the family inside will survive the initial fall, but then are faced with treacherous rushing rapids. They are probably frightened and ill-equipped to deal with the new challenges and dangers. The family relied on some occasional guidance and assistance before, but now they are desperate. Going back up the waterfall to the relatively calm river above simply is not an option.

As a grandparent, you are standing on the shore wondering what to do next. The fact you are reading this book indicates that you want to help. (Not all grandparents do want to help.) Should you stay on shore or jump in the water? Should you try to get in the boat, or would that make a crowded situation even worse? Should you run ahead and use your experience to warn them of hazards in the river they may not see? Why did they follow that channel in the river and get themselves into this situation anyway? Other people on shore are also shouting advice and trying to throw life lines and tools that might help the boat. Should you do the same or just get out of the way?

What is helpful?

INTRODUCTION

Setting the Scene

This book is directed toward grandparents and extended family members who sincerely want to understand and relate to children on the autism spectrum. Aunts, uncles, cousins as well as grandparents can be baffled by this affliction, and they often search to understand and discover ways to reach out both to the child and to overburdened parents. In reading about experiences of our family with our grandson as he grows from a beautiful two-year-old toddler to a six-foot-three-inch teenager, the reader will observe our heartaches as well as joyous moments found in grandparenting a child with autism.

A major impetus for writing this occurred after my first attendance at a Minnesota Autism Society conference in Minneapolis, when Micah was in preschool. Approximately 400 individuals were in attendance. There were exhibits by groups offering assistance, such as counseling for parents and education for children. Most in attendance listened to keynote speakers such as Temple Grandin, an adult with autism, now one of a few who can lead us into the mind of an autistic person. There were also small breakout sessions on topics from which attendees could choose. The facilitator at the session I chose asked for a show of hands from parents, therapists, teachers, and physicians. She was about to begin her discussion when I raised my hand. "Oh, who are you?" she queried.

"I am a grandparent."

"Well, how nice you could be here."

Nice, I thought, why aren't these rooms filled with grandparents? What a splendid opportunity to learn about autism!

Following the session a young mother approached me and tearfully asked, "How did your children convince you to come here? My parents insist my son does not have autism, and they refuse to discuss his circumstance with me. Now I must deal with my son's plight in addition to tension with my parents." I have since learned denial on the part of grandparents and extended family is not uncommon and can be a significant burden for young parents. If it is not denial, it may be intimidation or reluctance to become involved. Strained relationships with their children may leave grandparents estranged from their grandchildren.

That same day I stopped to view a large display of books about autism for sale. "Could you recommend a book that would be helpful, specifically for grandparents wanting to interact with their autistic grandchild?" I asked a salesperson. After some consideration she selected a book filled with pictures of cute kids.

"This is all we have. It would be a nice coffee table book for a grandparent."

Not only was there no book on grandparenting a child with autism, the book seller who was knowledgeable about autism had no concept of a need for such a book for grandparents. I concluded then that I should write the book I had in mind.

This book contains stories dealing with characteristics of our grandson, Micah, and is intended to show how my husband, Hollis, and I have interacted with him over a period of more than sixteen years. As a small boy, we dealt with severe communication issues, when he could not speak. There were the many Christmases when he could not deal with the confusion of gift opening around the lighted tree, and he would bolt into another room to be by himself. Then as a teenager he was able to speak quite well and ask, "When can I drive?" How does a grandparent respond to such a complicated issue?

There has been satisfaction as well as frustration during the years for our whole family, most especially for Micah's parents, Stuart and

Susan. Here, I want to emphasize an important observation that I have made: Parenting an autistic child is filled with stresses and strains not imagined by most of us. In addition, Micah's sister, Muriel, was often torn between love for her brother and inability to cope with the disruption he caused in her home and at school.

Hopefully, this book will encourage grandparents, extended family, and friends to lend a helping hand to parents of autistic children and thereby share in all the happy, sad, bizarre, and unique experiences that will ultimately enrich their family life.

Today's grandparents face a new and different world. Autism was rare when we were in school and even when we had young children. Our communities included children with autism, but the children may have been institutionalized or kept away from the mainstream. Today autism is on the cover of popular magazines, regularly in the news, and all over the internet. You do not need to look far, especially in public schools, to encounter children and families affected by autism. For some families, the fear of autism rivals the fear that past generations had of childhood diseases like polio and smallpox, now eradicated decades ago. Today increased resources for the study and treatment of autism provide much better support than was available for parents of children with autism before 1980.

Many books have been written about how parents, teachers, and other children can interact with autistic children. Grandparenting is different. We probably do not see our grandchildren every day and maybe not even every week, month, or year. We likely do not have any experience or training with autism. The relationship we want to develop with our grandchildren must be managed through the child's parents. The parent–grandparent relationship is layered with years of good and bad experiences that inevitably influence how we interact with our grandchildren. Of course, grandparents have advantages, too. As with all grandchildren, we can still spoil and have fun with our autistic grandchildren and then give them back to their parents before they start to get on our nerves.

It is important to recognize, as you read my stories, each child with autism is different. Autism today is described as a "spectrum disorder." Children with severe autism have almost no language capability or social skills. Children with mild autism have very few symptoms. People with mild autism are sometimes referred to as "high functioning." This means that people who do not know them well will likely not notice that they have autistic behaviors. Asperger Syndrome is a disorder where people have relatively mild sensory issues and limited social skills. At one time Asperger Syndrome was considered different than autism, but now it is recognized as a "high functioning" part of the autism spectrum. Autism Spectrum Disorder or ASD is the umbrella term used for all forms of autism and Asperger Syndrome.

Unlike some disorders, autism does not affect each individual the same way. Likewise, no two family situations are identical. A child's position on the autism spectrum may influence behavior and limit how much extended family members can be directly involved. In some situations, autism is only one physical or mental challenge facing the child, making involvement for grandparents more difficult. My intent is to encourage extended family members, especially grandparents, to engage themselves with their children and grandchildren to the greatest extent possible. At the very least we can show empathy for the journey challenging our children and can lend support simply by loving them. Involvement when appropriate is not only a way to be of assistance, but it also offers us opportunities for self-satisfaction and personal growth. For Hollis and me, there have been times to laugh and times to hold back tears. Our grandson is a special person; he must be accepted and loved as he is, not as we may have dreamed he would be.

Over the past twelve years, this book emerged in bits and pieces. Long delays occurred due to family crisis, health issues, and the normal pressures of living an active family life—creating frustrations over not completing the task. However, the desire to write never left. It gnawed in the back of my mind, calling me back to its completion. In retrospect, earlier I was not prepared to write a book about being the grandparent of a child on the autism spectrum. I lacked the necessary experience. Autistic behavior, I have learned, can be mysterious and unpredictable. Each new experience with my now sixteen-year-old grandson, Micah, provided insights helpful in dealing with our next involvement. I am still on a steep learning curve regarding autism. Early I viewed many interactions with Micah as frustrations, but I now know they were rich experiences, some filled with sadness, some with humor and joy.

There are a few conventions adopted for this book that the reader will notice. First, people with autism are always referred to with masculine pronouns (he, his, him, etc.). My grandson, Micah, appears throughout, therefore much of the text was necessarily written about a boy and using masculine pronouns seemed natural. Of course, there are also many girls with autism, but boys outnumber them by about four to one.

Second, the text is written as if the autistic child has two parents (one man, one woman) and four grandparents (two men, two women). This family model is probably the exception rather than the rule. But here again, consistency makes the text easier to read and follow, rather than trying to account for all possible family circumstances. No judgmental implications toward any family arrangements should be read into the text.

Third, the term "autistic person" is used as well as "person with autism." Several editors and the local autism society have suggested that "person with autism" is the most common usage at the time of publication of this book. It is likely the preferred words will change over time, much in the same way words like "colored" or "retarded" have fallen out of favor. If this book and its text appear dated in a few years, please know that we tried our best to incorporate commonly-used and widely-accepted language.

At the time this book was published, Micah was a tall high school junior, mainstreamed into public school. Life was not always easy for him, or so we perceive. In his own way, in the world into which he often escapes, he seemed happy.

The book ends with Micah approaching manhood. Obviously the story does not end there. Perhaps I will live to see how the story develops and be able to write again and tell you how Micah grew into a happy, productive member of society.

There is an unfortunate increase of autism in our society today, and with it a large cadre of caring grandparents. It is my wish that if you are part of such a growing group, you will find inspiration and enlightenment from this book.

DIAGNOSIS

The Journey Begins

Late one evening in 1998 I received an unforgettable telephone call from my son, Stuart. After a brief exchange of pleasantries, he said, "Mom, Susan and I need you and Dad on our team."

"What team is that?" I asked cautiously. Since I am not athletically inclined, I really did not care to be on any team.

"Micah has been diagnosed with autism. We will need your help."

Something like electric shocks ran through my body. I knew little about autism, but I did know there would likely be serious challenges ahead for Stuart's family. My beautiful, three-year-old grandson was not perfect. I wanted to cry.

On the other hand, there was some sense of relief. Now there was a diagnosis confirming that something was not right. His grandfather 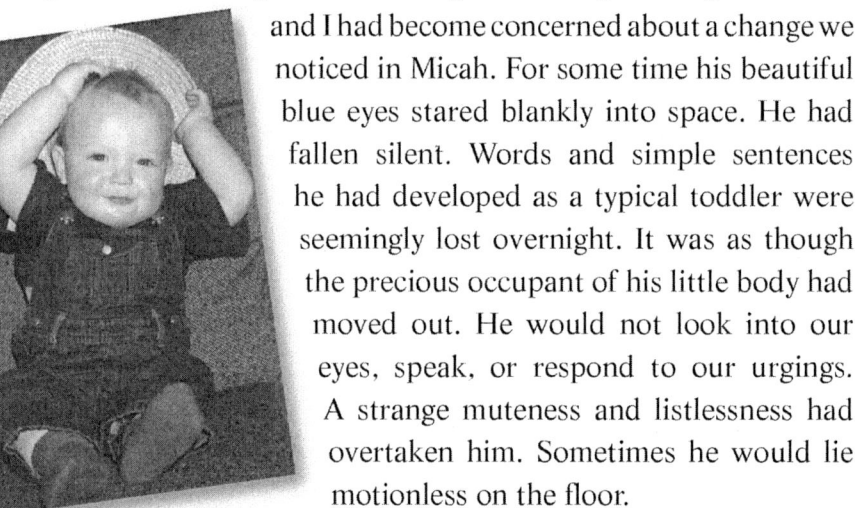 and I had become concerned about a change we noticed in Micah. For some time his beautiful blue eyes stared blankly into space. He had fallen silent. Words and simple sentences he had developed as a typical toddler were seemingly lost overnight. It was as though the precious occupant of his little body had moved out. He would not look into our eyes, speak, or respond to our urgings. A strange muteness and listlessness had overtaken him. Sometimes he would lie motionless on the floor.

Shaken, not knowing how we could help, I steadied my voice and said, "Of course, we want to be on your team. Tell me more."

Since this was all new to Stuart, there was little discussion that evening. It would be during the following days that bits and pieces of information about autism and treatment would dribble in to us.

I hung up the phone and shared my conversation with my husband. We were overwhelmed with concern for Micah, Stuart, Susan, and Micah's five-year-old sister, Muriel.

Slowly, plans for early intervention with special classes, speech and occupational therapies unfolded. As grandparents, we began to realize how we could fit the team and be of assistance. For example, we could drive Micah to and from the early education school in which he was enrolled. Therapy sessions were scheduled for him at various clinics in the metropolitan area, and transportation was needed. Since it is a problem finding qualified babysitters for a child with autism, we could be involved in child care.

Above all, we wanted to be there for this stricken family, to listen and to care.

We read books, attended conferences, searched the internet, and glued ourselves to the television when some mention was made of autism. We learned autism had become a world-wide challenge. One in every 110 children born in the United States is diagnosed with autism. It affects more boys than girls. Concerned friends sent newspaper and magazine clippings they found on the subject. Our family was not alone in this venture. Yet there were no answers to a question foremost in our minds, "Why Micah? What had caused this affliction?" But our journey with autism was underway. We had no idea where it would lead us.

DISCUSSION

The diagnosis of autism can be a scary thing. It can lead to feelings of fear and uncertainty because no one can predict how a child's autism will affect him and his family throughout his life. The diagnosis can also bring a sense of relief because the family can stop worrying about a myriad of other potential medical issues and begin to focus on autism.

We learned the symptoms of autism often start to appear before the child's first birthday. Physical and mental developments seem to plateau or regress. Many neuro-typical children display occasional regressions, and there is no reason to be alarmed. With autism, the regressions are pervasive and ongoing. Often only parents, grandparents, or an observant care provider may notice early signs of autism. Since these observers are not prepared to interpret those signs as autism, they often do not know to whom to turn or how alarmed they should be. Even consultation with doctors and special education professionals who can recognize symptoms of autism may not produce a diagnosis of autism. They see the child only occasionally and have no opportunity to observe day-to-day trends in behavior.

When our grandson was diagnosed with autism in the mid-1990s, the diagnosis was a long and drawn-out process. His parents did not tell us of their concern for Micah for many weeks. They started worrying when his speech regressed from five-word sentences to two-word sentences to no words at all. He stared at odd things like light bulbs. He began to shy away from other children and activities that he had previously enjoyed.

Stuart and Susan first discussed these early symptoms with their pediatrician. "Micah is probably fine," the doctor assured them. "I know his older sister is a real chatterbox. Boys usually develop their speech more slowly than girls do. He has probably just learned to let his sister do his talking for him. We'll see how he is doing at his next checkup."

Micah's parents were still concerned a few weeks later, so they scheduled appointments with an optometrist and an audiologist. Were physical problems with his eyes or ears causing his developmental regression, they wondered? Both doctors advertised that they tested young children. Unfortunately, they were overmatched against a child who would not follow instructions and who had a screaming aversion to any medical device. At least the doctors were gracious enough to not charge for the harrowing half hour in their office. Micah's parents did not seek out other eye doctors or ear doctors. He passed simple tests at home, such as responding when he heard soft noises and spotting favorite toys across the room. His sight and hearing seemed to be just fine.

The medical school at a local university had a department of pediatric neuroscience. There was great demand for their services, so appointments for initial consultations had to be scheduled months in advance. Micah was put on the waiting list, and finally the date arrived. Because of the program's specialization and reputation, everyone was hopeful that the cause of Micah's behavior would finally be diagnosed. Upon arriving at the clinic office, hope began to fade. The sparsely furnished waiting room contained no toys or anything of interest to a child. Appointments were running late, so Susan had to sit in this bleak room for over four hours while trying to entertain an irritable child with only the few items she happened to bring along in the diaper bag.

When the exam finally started, the doctor was clearly incapable of establishing any rapport with the child. He clumsily went through a series of tests, and Micah was in no mood to participate or cooperate. The doctor tried to get him to engage in pretend play with little teddy bears. Micah refused. Micah's mom explained that Micah did not like bears, but if there were stuffed pigs, monkeys, or elephants, Micah would probably play with them. The doctor told her, "Be quiet. You don't know anything about this."

In another test, the doctor wanted to see if Micah exhibited any understanding or concern for another person's feelings. The doctor pretended to stub his toe on a table leg and complained that it hurt. Micah looked at him as if to say, "You are the worst actor I have ever seen. Even if you were hurt, I am not sure that I would want to stay in this room long enough to help you."

After this first appointment, the university clinic suggested Micah had speech aphasia, a language processing disorder often associated with brain damage. His parents quickly looked for information about aphasia and found many of Micah's symptomatic behaviors were consistent with this diagnosis. However, many behaviors were not. They discussed the diagnosis with a speech therapist at the Early Childhood Special Education (ECSE) school Micah had started attending. The therapist felt it was a wrong diagnosis and suggested being patient until more tests were performed.

Another appointment with the university program was scheduled a few weeks later. A second doctor reviewed the earlier test results and performed some additional tests. This time the diagnosis was that Micah had speech dyspraxia, a physical inability to use his facial muscles to form words and make sounds. Again his parents began to gather information and discuss the diagnosis with speech therapists. His speech therapists at ESCE disagreed with the diagnosis. A third appointment at the university did not yield any other diagnosis.

Micah's parents were growing more and more frustrated by the various professionals' inability to reach a consensus about their son's condition. At the same time they were becoming increasingly concerned about his lack of developmental progress. Finally they asked his ESCE teacher, "If it's not aphasia and not dyspraxia, then what do you think is affecting Micah?"

The teacher was hesitant to respond because she was not a doctor. After some more prodding and promises not to put all our faith in her opinion, she replied, "It looks like autism to me. The school district has a relationship with Sheila Merzer. Perhaps she could evaluate Micah and tell you if it is autism."

Dr. Sheila Merzer had done some of the earliest research on autism in Minnesota in the 1970s. Back then, she had scoured the state to find six children with autism to include in her original study. Today she could probably find six students with autism in any large high school, a testament to the dramatic rise in the occurrence of autism. Dr. Merzer agreed to see Micah.

As was the case with other doctors specializing in childhood development disorders, the appointment with Dr. Merzer had to be scheduled many weeks in advance. Micah's parents had time to research and learn the basics about autism. They learned that not all children with autism behave the same way and behavior associated with autism can start and stop throughout a child's development.

At this early stage, when Micah was about three years old, he did not have repetitive behaviors such as rapid hand movements or pacing. Those came later. He was very empathetic and aware of other people's feelings, two characteristics many autistic children lack. Micah liked to "snuggle" with his family. He did not exhibit "mind blindness," the inability to perceive what others may be thinking. All of this probably contributed to the doctors not recognizing Micah's autism.

When Dr. Merzer met with Micah, it was in a play room at his school. She started by observing Micah playing with some toys by himself for several minutes. She then introduced herself to Micah and tried to engage him in some play activities. Micah plainly rejected her friendly advances, so Dr. Merzer backed off and let him play by himself a while longer. Later she was able to interact with Micah and perform some simple tests.

Dr. Merzer's diagnosis arrived a few days later. She concluded Micah had moderate to severe autism. She noted his autistic behaviors and said others might develop over time. Her diagnosis and prognosis were not perfect. For example, Micah often "jabbered," making unfamiliar sounds in a high falsetto or squeaky voice. Dr. Merzer was confident he would stop using the high voice by the time he was eight or nine years old, as his vocal chords continued to develop. That did not happen.

The autism diagnosis hit Micah's family and teachers with a very soft thud. On one hand, it was troubling to hear that he had a disorder for which there was no known cure and which he would never outgrow. On the other hand, it was good to have a word that they could all use to discuss Micah's issues. They could all direct efforts toward a common and better-defined purpose, share ideas with others who had experienced autism, and embrace the "autism community" that would help support Micah.

This story of Micah's diagnosis is not meant to disparage the medical community. Remember, this story took place in the mid-1990s when the autism epidemic was just beginning to be noticed and before autism had been featured on the covers of most news magazines. Standard methods for diagnosing autism had been developed for pediatricians only a few years earlier. The doctors who did not recognize Micah's autism were not negligent; they just lacked the specialized skills and experience needed to effectively work with young children with autism. However, with the prevalence of autism in today's world, every pediatrician and special education provider should know about autism. If you encounter one that does not, Micah's parents advise finding a doctor or educator who does know about autism.

The experience of Micah's diagnosis highlights the importance of the observations of parents, grandparents, day care providers, teachers, and others who see a child on a regular basis. The early signs of autism are often subtle and may not always be present during a brief visit to a doctor's office. The progression of autistic behaviors over a longer period of time can be vital to recognizing the disorder.

Often, parents are resistant to having a child evaluated and diagnosed. The reasons are many and are understandable. Some parents may be in denial, consciously or subconsciously refusing to acknowledge that their child may have a disability. They may feel labeling the child as autistic will cause themselves or other people to view the child as less appealing and less desirable to be around. Other parents may fear a diagnosis would be detrimental to the child by enabling preferential treatment and imposing the burden of low expectations throughout childhood. Still others may believe the symptoms are not caused by autism, but by some other condition with which they have more familiarity or experience.

Financial factors can play a role in seeking a diagnosis. Insurance plans may not cover visits to specialists, especially if the primary care physician does not agree that an evaluation for autism is warranted. If the family has no health insurance or cannot afford co-pays, parents may become hesitant in ordering a diagnosis.

The important thing to remember about an autism diagnosis is that the parents, to a large extent, can control how it is used. They may find it advantageous to let everyone know. They may try to keep it confidential among family members until such time that they become comfortable with the new situation in their lives.

Micah's parents have learned the autism diagnosis and label are tools that can be used in different ways. The diagnosis is a requirement for eligibility to many government-sponsored and school-sponsored programs. The programs can include financial aid, medical coverage, speech and occupational therapy, educational alternatives, and a variety of activities not available to children without a diagnosis.

When requesting unusual accommodations at a restaurant, doctor's office, friend's house, etc., it is often useful to simply state that a child has autism. Most people, even if they do not know what autism is, will then try to work out the accommodations because they understand it is a medical condition and not just bad behavior.

WHAT GRANDPARENTS CAN DO

The first thing grandparents can do is educate themselves about autism. The internet abounds with websites about autism. Starting with short, general articles, they can work their way up to longer, more detailed articles and books. Most libraries stock a shelf or two of books pertaining to autism.

Grandparents may want to explore their own feelings about autism and disabilities in general. How will an autism diagnosis change the feelings they have toward their children and grandchildren? This topic will be discussed more in later chapters of this book. Coming to grips with their own feelings may help them become more understanding and responsive to their son or daughter's parenting practices and how best to inform and include extended family members in the journey.

Grandparents informed about autism are better prepared to be supportive and recognize the stress that comes with an autism diagnosis. Parents receive information and advice from many different directions. They may react in ways that seem illogical to unprepared grandparents.

Our family has found children with autism require a greater time commitment than typical children. Doctors' and specialists' appointments take large amounts of time and energy. Often transportation to a specialist's office is a challenge in itself. Consequently, parents can really use assistance with time-consuming chores. Taking care of their other children for a half day or longer can be a big help. Housekeeping, yard work, and cooking are good grandparent chores.

Before he was three years old, Micah enrolled in an Early Childhood Special Education (ECSE) program sponsored by the local public school district. In addition, he participated in private speech, physical, and occupational therapy. His grandfather and I were privileged to drive him to some of those classes and observe through one-way glass windows. The lessons seemed intense for so small a child, but as a result we witnessed positive changes in him. We were looking into Micah's world, but we knew the film on the glass had to dissolve so he could begin looking into ours.

As grandparents, what can we do to help Micah?" we queried a therapist.

"Do everything you can to draw him out of his world into yours. Play and tussle with him, just as you would other children, and don't give up," the therapist responded. It was a powerful suggestion, serving us well today and, I suspect, well into his adulthood. It means treating him, as much as possible, as you would other children and adults in all aspects of his life.

Autism can cause considerable financial stress. Some doctors and clinics may not be covered by the parents' insurance plan. Others require initial payment in full, with later reimbursement (hopefully) by the insurance company. Doctors' services are usually available only during limited hours, so the parents may need to take time off from work to go to extra appointments. Mental stress runs high in families dealing with autism, and financial concerns can be a major contributor to that stress. Grandparents who can help financially or assist in some way to reduce expenses can aid with relieving stress. Sources for funding may be available, but researching funding is time consuming. Grandparents often have extra time to assist with this process.

SENSORY ISSUES

A Christmas Party

When Micah was three, my daughter-in-law Susan called and asked, "Could you escort Micah to his school's Christmas party? Both Stu and I have to work."

"Yes, I'd love to," was my eager response. "I want to help in any way I can."

On the appointed day I drove to the parking lot of a one-story school building. Micah wanted to run ahead of me, but I held his hand firmly, hoping not to slip on hard-packed snow. We were just inside the door when he turned and, with a terrified look, tried to run back to the car. He was unable to express himself, but I knew crowds of adults with strange faces, loud voices, and boisterous laughing were not part of his school experience. I carried his stiff, struggling body back into the hallway and managed to remove our coats.

We were greeted by Mrs. Johns, his teacher. She explained the party program: "Go from room to room and do activities set up at various stations. You will find puzzles, building blocks, and pictures to color—all things Micah loves. The last room has cookies, drinks, and Santa Claus."

"What fun," I chirped, taking Micah's hand.

Just inside the first room, Micah stopped, looked at a seeming wall of people, and bolted down the hallway. When I caught his hand, he pulled me into a room filled with large plastic toys and slammed the door shut. The room looked off limits for the day. It was quiet, and we were alone. Silently, he began riding little cars, rolling on large balls, and sliding down a small slide. He was happy; I was perplexed.

In a short while, a promise of cookies lured him toward the Santa Claus room. As we approached, he covered his noise-sensitive ears, blocking out laughter and conversation. Micah screamed when Santa approached him and ran back to the off-limits room, Grandma in pursuit. Inside our sanctuary, we ate cookies I had managed to grab and calmed ourselves. I was also beginning to appreciate this place of refuge.

I was seated on a child-size chair, thinking we would leave the party, when suddenly Mrs. Johns opened the door, "Are you having trouble getting Micah to join the festivities?"

"Well, it is not my idea to hide in here. Yes, he is afraid of the crowd and of Santa Claus. What can I do?" I was ashamed of my pleading voice. As a grandmother, I had failed.

"This is my fault," Mrs. Johns voice was consoling. "Micah is accustomed to following a picture map, or story board, as a daily routine. In all the commotion, it was forgotten. I will get it for you, if you would like it."

"Please, yes! And, thank you." Relief washed over me.

Mrs. Johns returned with a cloth upon which small pictures of activities and room numbers were attached to Velcro strips. Micah looked once at the first picture and room number, then was off, weaving around legs and children, to room number one. It was amazing! Activity one was completed and that picture was removed from the board; then we went on to room two, and eventually ten. I merely watched and followed as my grandson darted from room to room. We skipped the Santa Claus festivities, donned our coats, and left. Micah had enjoyed the party on his own terms. He was happy, and so was Grandma.

DISCUSSION

The Christmas party presented Micah with a number of sensory issues I now know are common among autistic children. Micah, being three years old, was not aware his behavior was in any way unusual. At that time, I was unfamiliar with many characteristics of autism and was at a loss about how to help Micah cope with situations encountered at the party.

Everyone reacts to sensory inputs. Smells of cookies baking can draw us toward the kitchen, while sounds of fingernails on a blackboard may make us cringe and move away. Autistic children develop attractions and aversions to sensory inputs differently than neurotypical children. Sounds, smells, tastes, textures, and light sources that might be quite pleasant to most people can be unpleasant or even painful to an autistic child. You probably know someone who has an unusual like or dislike, for instance, for a particular food. Children with autism have likes and dislikes too, but they are often so unusual or exaggerated that they interfere with their everyday activities.

Similarly, everyone reacts to social situations as well. Remember when you were a kid? You would approach a group of kids younger than you differently than you would approach a group of kids older than you. Some people, groups, and situations seem to invite us, others make us want to get away fast.

People with autism prefer familiar places and social settings and may have a strong aversion to changes. Neurotypical people often have the same preferences, but it is raised to an extreme in autism.

When Micah approached his preschool on the night of the Christmas party, he was eagerly anticipating seeing the teachers and other children he saw there every school day. Instead, Micah saw people he did not recognize, and it made him fearful. Through years of experience, I have found that Micah is much more at ease if he knows who will be in the room ahead of time. More information is always better. He likes to know the names and relationships of people. If names are not known, he likes to know something about the person (i.e. this person is a teacher, that person is a friend of your cousin). Even if they are complete strangers, Micah prefers knowing who will be there, rather than encountering an unexpected person, group, or crowd.

Micah was anticipating doing the things he liked to do at school, preferably in the order he normally did them. Although the puzzles, toys, and craft supplies were all there, they were surrounded by strange people and there was no order or schedule. Many people with autism need to have a routine. Disruptions to routine can be very troubling. In Micah's case, he can handle variations to his routines, but it is much better if the variations are explained to him ahead of time.

Micah functions much better when an activity is organized visually. It seems that he can do assignments if they are arranged and scheduled on a story board. Special education teachers use storyboards, also known as Picture Exchange Communication Systems (PECS) They consist of simple pictures, symbols, or icons that denote different places, things, people, and actions. Some examples are:

snack

bathroom

break

Symbols are arranged in order so the child can see what to do next and what is coming in the future. At school, Micah's teachers made up a variety of these symbols with Velcro tags on the back and arranged them on a piece of felt. The symbols are arranged for a particular task (i.e. wash hands, then get cookies and milk, then clean up) or for an entire day (i.e. story time, then snacks, then play time, and so on.) At home, his parents made laminated storyboards that helped with routine tasks, especially personal hygiene. Symbols can also be arranged into "to-do" lists or "first–then" boards to encourage and reward various tasks. Lists are important to most people with autism. I have heard an adult with autism tell he required lists just to complete daily tasks such as combing hair, brushing teeth, preparing and eating breakfast.

Micah was terrified of Santa Claus at the Christmas party, and that did not change as he grew older. Many children see Santa as a large, loud, strangely-dressed, odd-looking, and terribly frightening individual.

The crowd at the Christmas party presented Micah with loud, uncomfortable noise. Some people with autism have sensitive hearing. This may lend itself to unusual abilities, like musical talent, but it can also be a disability. In Micah's case, loud voices, especially in unison, are particularly irritating. A crowd singing the national anthem or even his family saying grace together at the dinner table is very irritating to his ears. Most children, especially boys, love being in the crowd at a sporting event. These outings often ended early for Micah's family with Micah crying in agony because of the crowd noise. Eventually Micah simply refused to enter a gymnasium or sports arena.

Micah also has an interesting relationship to elephant noises. He has loved elephants since he was very young. His room is filled with elephant posters, elephant models, elephant books, and a three-foot-tall stuffed elephant. Yet, Micah cannot tolerate the trumpeting sound of an elephant. He watches television shows about elephants with great interest. But when they make a trumpeting noise, he runs from the room holding his ears. He then peeks around the corner at the television to see if it is safe to come back into the room. He also has demonstrated this sensitivity at a zoo. When Micah's family visited the zoo in Kansas City, the entrance was at the opposite side of the park from the elephants. Micah immediately announced, "I can hear the elephants calling me," and pointed in the direction of the elephant enclosure. The background noise of parents and kids and some nearby birds were all other family members could hear. When they finally located the elephants, Micah approached the enclosure, holding his ears, with a visible combination of fascination and fear.

Fortunately, Micah's sensitivity to certain loud noises has a simple remedy—earplugs. Micah's mom keeps a supply of inexpensive earplugs in her purse, ready for any occasion. At first he had to have an adult put the plugs in his ears, but he soon learned to do it himself, and he is happy when the plugs are available.

The loud noises and intense visual images in movie theaters can also be irritating. Many movie theaters now hold special screenings for people, especially kids, with sensory issues. The volume of the movie is turned down, the house lights are left on, and no one complains if someone has to move around or leave the theater. Interestingly, in recent years, Micah has declined to attend these special screenings. Tolerating the noise of the movies seems to be one of his ways of proving he is grown up, self-sufficient, and normal, although sometimes his discomfort is still obvious.

WHAT GRANDPARENTS CAN DO

Grandparents can be aware that children with autism may have extreme reactions to certain sensory stimuli. When other children may find certain situations mildly unpleasant, children with autism may experience genuine physical discomfort or pain. Ideally, the child's parents should identify these issues to the grandparents if the parents can anticipate the situation being a problem. However, this is practically impossible, given the number of sensory issues that are often present. It can also lead to an unnecessary suppression of fun activities, because the grandparents want to avoid a problem. A better solution is for the grandparents to be ready to react and cope with the sensory issues as they arise.

As grandparents, we can stock supplies that will help a child with autism cope with sensory issues. Some are common things almost everyone needs, such as sunscreen or sunglasses. Others are less common, like earplugs or disposable gloves for children with textural issues. Food issues and allergies are discussed in another chapter.

When taking a grandchild with autism somewhere, especially somewhere they have not been before, talking to them about what they will experience can be helpful. Explain where you are going, who will be there, and what likely will happen. Hopefully, your grandchild will warn you if anything sounds unpleasant. Then you have some time to think of a solution or response.

Following a child's established routines and schedule as much as possible can be beneficial. If a deviation is necessary, explain it ahead of time and make clear why it is necessary. Clarifying an upcoming situation more than once can save some stressful occurrences. Some children with autism receive verbal instructions and explanations very well, but some will not. Visual stories and prompts may work better. If you have a little bit of artistic talent or at least some ability, you could try drawing your own simple storyboards. If you want some help, there are many sources of symbols for common tasks, including at www.symbolworld.org, www.pureclipart.com, and www.abaresources.com/free.htm.

Children with autism may refuse to do something for reasons that are not apparent, or for reasons that seem completely irrational. At times no amount of preparation, bribery, pleading, or accommodation will change their minds. Is this bad behavior or just a product of autism? Every child and every situation deserves case-by-case consideration. It is important to remember facts and rules are often different for one child with autism than they are for other children. At the root of the situation there may be very real sensory issues unique to one grandchild, but not another. There are therapies and techniques that can help people with autism overcome some disabling problems. As grandparents, with limited time with a child, we need to learn to cope with behavior as it is today.

The Christmas party so long ago was a huge learning experience for me. Because of the frustrations I dealt with that cold December day, I plunged into an ever-unfolding adventure of learning more about the autistic mind.

LANGUAGE CHALLENGES

"I Couldn't Have Done It Without You"

When leaving our home after an overnight stay, Micah's Mom asked, "Micah, did you say thank you to Grandma and Grandpa?"

"Thank you, Grandma. I couldn't have done it without you."

What a curious expression from a nine year old, one might think. However, it was a good example of Micah having heard a phrase he memorized and now using in a seemingly inappropriate way. This is just one of many problems facing an autistic mind.

At seventeen months, Micah lost all language skills. He was taught to speak again, beginning at two and one-half years of age. It was a slow tedious process on the part of speech therapists, parents, friends, and relatives.

The hundreds of idioms, turned phrases, and expressions we use daily are confusing to autistic children because they tend to think very literally. Imagine trying to explain "beating around the bush," "an axe to grind," or "bottom of the totem pole" to someone understanding words at face value. Some phrases that have been difficult for Micah are "under the weather," "raining cats and dogs," and "in one ear and out the other." During a conversation with Micah's then sixteen-year-old-sister, his mom cautioned that she not "shoot herself in the foot" when making a decision. Micah became agitated, concerned his sister had a gun and she might use it.

This dilemma of language for Micah is akin to learning a foreign language. The vocabulary and sentence structure may be perfected, but the humorous expressions and colloquialisms are confusing. After falling off his bicycle and receiving minor injuries, Micah once exclaimed, "I lead a dog's life!"

As a teenager, the jargon of his contemporaries is an obstacle and limits his already challenged social skills with peer groups. Micah has received instruction in idiom understanding as part of speech therapy sessions. Therapists attempt to explain the meaning of words he hears from his classmates, some of which can be confusing even to adults who do not have autism.

However, it is evident that Micah can be trained to use idioms. At the age of thirteen and nearly six feet tall, he enjoyed saying, "I'm not knee-high to a grasshopper anymore."

At age fourteen we were thrilled with a response from Micah to an idiom used by his father. During a conversation with a friend, his dad said, "It's no longer a secret that our daughter is going to Europe after her graduation. Someone let the cat out of the bag."

"Oh, you mean someone spilled the beans?" Micah unexpectedly interjected. Such moments of understanding, as if he is looking into the window of the real world, are a joy to the ears of Micah's family.

DISCUSSION

At times, the innocence of people on the autism spectrum can be refreshing, but it can lead to possible serious consequences. Caution is required because immature and thoughtless peers sometimes tease a person with autism who has misunderstood some teenage jargon. This is painful for those who care deeply about the person with autism. Note that same innocence can protect the autistic child from feeling embarrassed or even understanding they are being ridiculed.

Another facet of literal interpretation is adherence to television commercials and the dire outcomes if certain instructions are not followed. We have all been warned that if we don't act within two days, this offer will run out and we will spend the rest of our life suffering the consequences! Micah will feverishly copy a phone number and insist his parents order the product advertised, immediately.

There are therapeutic classes available to help persons with autism understand the myriad of idioms, colloquial expressions, and jargons that are an important facet of our language. Micah has received much help in this realm at Courage Center, a non-profit organization offering physical and educational assistance for challenged children and adults. His teachers and para-professionals in the Stillwater school system have helped greatly over the years as well.

Micah enjoys non-fiction books much more than fiction. Perhaps he chooses non-fiction because fiction often requires imagination, but non-fiction is to be taken literally. Books about animals (especially dinosaurs), insects, snakes, and outer space are his choice over any storybook, even classic children stories. The *National Geographic* is his favorite magazine.

Language skills, awareness of acceptable conversations, are a challenge to Micah, but he is learning and improving.

WHAT GRANDPARENTS CAN DO

Be cautious of language used around grandchildren with autism. Speak slowly and explain meanings of expressions or idioms when a child seems puzzled or obviously does not understand a sentence with an idiom included.

You can explain to other family members and friends that children with autism often take expressions literally.

When remarks made by your autistic grandchild are unintentionally amusing, do not laugh as you might with other grandchildren. Children with autism can at times seem oblivious to such laughter, but at other times they may become emotional from such attention.

If your grandchild enjoys having you read to him, try books that incorporate idioms and explain them as you read. You could compile a list of idioms and colloquial expressions common to your locality, and choose one to discuss with him when you are together.

INTERPERSONAL RELATIONSHIPS

Micah Shares Valentines

Cupid is very much present in elementary classrooms on Valentine's Day. That chubby little cherub of Greek mythology, with quiver of arrows and bow at ready, often transforms even the meanest, toughest boy in the back row of a classroom.

Micah arrived home one day early in February with a list of his sixth grade classmates in his backpack. His skinny, gangly frame hardly evoked thoughts of Cupid, and his aloof personality did not stimulate a warm feeling generally associated with Valentine's Day. However, his parents were elated! Micah was enthused about joining the frivolity of the forthcoming holiday. Written instructions accompanied the list from his teacher, Mrs. Nelson. "If you place a card to anyone in our Valentine box, you must include one for everyone in the class, so no one will feel left out."

During his early years, Micah was not interested in exchanging Valentines. His limited social skills prevented him from understanding or enjoying such exchanges. He functioned in his own world, oblivious to the pleasures of expressing affection. Now, however, it seemed he was slowly emerging from his cocoon.

Having already selected Valentines for his classmates, with much coaching from his mom, Micah now set about the task of addressing his cards. Mom frequently checked on his progress, thinking how wonderful it was that he wanted to do this by himself. There was the possibility Micah was focused on completing a task rather than thinking of the party aspects as an outcome of his efforts. He was working slowly and laboriously, printing names in large, irregular letters. She noted one Valentine addressed, "To Micah," signed "From Micah."

"Why are you sending a card to yourself?" she inquired.

"Because Mrs. Nelson said to send to everyone on the list."

This was obviously Micah's autistic mind interpreting instructions very literally, but it also brought to my mind the adage, "To love others, you must first love yourself."

DISCUSSION

People with autism seem to process language and ideas differently than other people. This is generally a challenge in everyday life, but it can also be an advantage. Most often, it leads to confusion and difficulties when interacting with others. But it can also bring insight on ordinary occurrences and even lead to brilliant advancements in the arts, sciences, engineering, and other human endeavors.

Micah's challenge with the Valentine instructions illustrates the Theory of Mind that is usually severely underdeveloped in people with autism. The Theory of Mind is the ability to understand what others are seeing and thinking. It typically develops in children between the ages of three and five. In children with autism, Theory of Mind develops much later or may never develop. This is often described as "mind-blindness."

The classic experiment used to describe and diagnose mind-blindness involves three people in a room. The person conducting the test shows the others a ball sitting on a table with a large box and a small box. The tester takes the ball and puts it in the large box. Next, one person leaves the room. The tester takes the ball from the large box and puts it into the small box. The tester asks the remaining person, "Where will the other person look for the ball when they come back in the room?" A typical person would respond that they will look in the large box, because that is where they last saw it. A person with autism would reply that they would look in the small box, because they should also know that the ball was shifted. Because the person with autism lacks the Theory of Mind, they think everyone has the same information and experiences they do. They cannot distinguish or understand the person outside the room has had a different experience and therefore a different understanding and perspective on the situation.

When Micah followed the Valentine instructions to the letter, he was incapable of understanding exactly what the teacher wanted. He could not put himself in her shoes to figure out that she wanted everyone to receive the same number of Valentines, not that she wanted him to write one to himself. He had not developed the Theory of Mind necessary to follow the teacher's adequate, but not perfect, instructions.

An interesting implication of the Theory of Mind is that many children with autism seem incapable of lying. Even as a teenager, Micah almost always tells the truth, even when it is not to his advantage to do so. Micah will say things like, "My stomach doesn't feel so good right now." When asked, "Is that because you are sick or because you don't want to do your homework?" he will answer truthfully, "It's because I don't want to do homework." He knows that genuine sickness is an effective excuse for getting out of homework. We would like to think that this is an outward sign of outstanding moral character—and perhaps it is—but there is something at the root of that character, and it is probably related to the autism. It is not formed by parental discipline, because his parents have never caught him in a lie or discussed lying with him. It is more related to mind-blindness, believing everyone has the same knowledge you do. Lying about a stomach ache does not make sense to Micah, because he assumes everyone knows as well as he does that his stomach feels fine.

The inability to tell a lie can be endearing, but it can also have unfortunate social consequences. When someone with autism says, "My mom can't come to the phone right now because it sounds like she's going to the bathroom," or "Your new haircut really looks weird," it can be embarrassing or even harmful. They may say these things because they lack the Theory of Mind and assume everyone sees and thinks what they see and think. It also may be the underdevelopment of a filter that allows most people to refrain from saying damaging or inappropriate things that pop into their minds.

It should be noted, some parents report their children with autism are quite good liars. But for many other children with autism, the improvement of lying skills can be seen as a cognitive milestone in their development!

One can only imagine the potential pitfalls that face children with autism as they enter adulthood. Teenage dating is already awkward and filled with enough strange mind games without having one person in the relationship playing by a different set of rules. People with autism may say or not say things because they assume the other person is already thinking the same as they are.

When people with autism get a job, the challenges of following instructions and relating to co-workers can be difficult, but manageable with proper training. Employees with autism may interpret work assignments in strange ways, and they may be oblivious to what their co-workers are silently thinking about their appearance or behavior. At the same time, employers can take advantage of the attention to detail, the willingness to do repetitive tasks, and the fresh perspectives people with autism bring to their jobs.

The challenge in communicating with autistic children is to concentrate on specific details and be complete in descriptions, and not to anticipate anything more than asked. We should not limit the challenge by assuming the child is not capable because he is autistic, rather we should be ready for spectacular performance. Limiting our expectations can be limiting the child's opportunity to excel.

WHAT GRANDPARENTS CAN DO

Difficulty communicating over the span of two generations can be a common dilemma for all well-intending grandparents. Add to this the complications of autism and communicating becomes especially challenging. Recognizing a child's tendency toward literal interpretation is important, but not likely intuitive. Thus grandparents may do well to keep this characteristic foremost in their minds when interacting with a grandchild with autism.

Grandparents should stay alert to the possibility of a child's confusion with instructions or even conversation, and be prepared to provide clarifying information. Being on the alert for confusing statements by others in the presence of your grandchild and making clarification can save him from difficult situations. Helping other family members and friends understand a literal-thinking child increases everyone's comfort level. The Valentines story deals with literal interpretation characteristics, but also shows that Micah can interact socially if given a comfortable opportunity. Grandparents can foster such opportunities. Help the child write cards to other family members. Read instructions for games and then follow them. Play hide and go seek (recommended to help mind-blindness). Erase the idea that "if I can't see them, they can't see me."

COMMUNICATION

Taylor Emails Micah

"Hey Micah! Want to play catch?"

"NO!"

"Come on, we'll pitch it slow."

"NO."

These words rose from the front lawn at our Wisconsin home, with Lake Mallalieu shimmering in the background. It is August. Our grandchildren Taylor, Connor, and Hannah are visiting from Kansas City for a week. Taylor is sixteen, Connor thirteen, and Hannah is eight years old. Micah at age nine has been anticipating the visit of his cousins. He sees them only once or twice a year and talks excitedly about their arrival, weeks in advance. Now, he is unable to even look them in the eye, his shyness allowing only, "yes" or "no" to questions.

Micah with his cousins at an earlier age.

Micah has traveled with his family from their home thirty minutes away. While the boys play catch, carefully aiming away from the lake, Micah clearly wants to be near them. He paces back and forth in the driveway, nervously shaking his hands. It is difficult for a grandparent to witness, knowing this grandchild is yearning to play, but an inhibition within holds him back. It is a powerful inhibition no one understands or can break through at this point in his life.

Fast forward five years to 2010. Micah is a fourteen-year-old ninth grader. Years of speech and physical therapy, mainstreaming in public school, and accomplishments with computers have created changes in Micah's life. He is still shy, has difficulty making eye contact, and is intimidated around his cousins. They continue making attempts to draw him into conversation or games, but find only watching television with him is successful. However, Taylor, now a twenty-one-year old junior at UCLA and a wide receiver on the football team, has tried communicating with Micah through a contemporary means, e-mails. It is working. Following are examples of their communications, without editing.

E-mail from Taylor:

> Hey Micah, It was really great seeing Grandma and Grandpa and Muriel at the game. I haven't seen your sister in a very long time. On Saturday you have to be sure to wear the shirt we picked out for you at the UCLA bookstore, because that is the day of our big game with USC, our biggest rival. Some students from USC came to our campus last night and dumped red and yellow paint all over the statue of our school mascot. The director of *Transformers* said a third movie will be kind of scary. I want to see it, but we will have to wait a whole year. Love, Taylor.

E-mail from Micah:

> Hi, I wore the shirt. I like it and it fits. I will wear it on Saturday, what time is your game on? The other students dumped paint on the statue of your mascot that's not good. You better tell your principal to call their school and tell their principal that they are in big trouble. The third *Transformers* movie won't freak me out. When will the preview come out? Love, Micah.

E-mail from Taylor:

> Hey Micah, how have you been? How's school going? I just got back from Las Vegas. We saw the Beatles Cirque de

Communication | 43

Soleil; it was crazy. People flipping and flying everywhere to Beatles music. Have you ever heard of the Beatles? I bought a CD of their music and I love it. Talk to you soon. Love, Taylor.

E-mail response from Micah:

Hey Taylor, I had been a little crummy. School was getting hard for me. I never heard of the Beatles. Some people can't do flips, and people don't really fly. So how did they flip and fly? For spring break, I'm going to Arizona and Texas. You still haven't told me when the 3rd Transformers is coming out. Talk to you soon. Micah.

E-mail from Taylor:

Hey Micah. Yeah, I've been to Texas. You will have fun there for spring break. Do you know what part of Texas you will visit? I just looked up when Transformers 3 comes out and it will be July 1, 2011, more than a year away. How is the weather in Minnesota? I was back in Kansas recently and the weather was horrible, it was freezing. I can't wait for summer to get here. Love, Taylor.

E-mail response from Micah:

Hi Taylor, I will have fun in Texas on spring break. I don't know what part of Texas I will visit. I don't get it. I thought Transformers 3 is this year. We have a lot of snow here. Did you have a snow storm? Summer doesn't start until May. Love, Micah.

Will this electronic exchange help Micah to have a conversation with Taylor next time they meet, or will he continue to look away and retreat to another room? Time will tell.

DISCUSSION

Several characteristics of Micah and other teens with autism are brought to the forefront in this story.

Micah will still pace back and forth and shake his hands when nervous or not occupied with a distraction such as television, or activity of special interest, such as visiting a museum. At times he may laugh and talk to himself while pacing and shaking his hands. This is referred to as stimming.

Fixations on a subject such as Micah's obsession with Transformers seem to be common among people with autism. He collected Transformers figures, collected DVDs of *Transformers* movies, and at times wanted to talk of nothing else. At age eight he wanted to own every Dr. Seuss book in print. For years, long after kids his age stopped doing this, he collected dinosaur figures, books, and DVDs, dragging these items with him everywhere. Because of that intense interest, he hopes to go on a dinosaur dig some day with his parents.

As Micah progresses through his teen years, social skills still do not come easily. Sometimes it is difficult to know if his lack in skills is because of his autism or because he is a teenager—for example, letting a door slam into the person walking behind him or protesting loudly when his parents ask him to perform even a simple task.

Micah at age 10.

He is neat and orderly with his clothing and possessions, but is slow developing personal hygiene habits. He will converse with persons well known to him, but prefers to answer questions rather than initiate any conversation. Micah is not physically confrontational and will quickly say, "I'm sorry," if he perceives he has done harm to anyone.

At age sixteen, Micah's speech is improving, and he at times will respond in sentences to questions. In his emails with Taylor there is obvious, ongoing improvement in sentence structure and spelling.

Micah communicates in many different ways, some with more success than others. His verbal skills remain far behind his age level despite weekly speech therapy sessions. This is not to say that speech therapy has not been beneficial, but it would be surprising if his speech ever approaches a typical person's abilities. His speech therapists have taught him to introduce himself to someone with a confident handshake and a sincere-sounding, "It is nice to meet you." He is also getting better at ordering in restaurants by waiting his turn and then ordering chicken fingers and French fries.

Micah has always exhibited better listening skills than ability to speak. He is more able to take in sounds, words, and information than to get them back out again. Micah is not a savant who takes in and memorizes vast amounts of information. In fact, he does not seem to retain as much information as typical people. However, his abilities in this area are far greater than his abilities to speak or write. When given a complex command like, "Go to the garage, look in the cabinet behind the bicycles, and bring a Philips-head screwdriver," he can complete the task without assistance. But he would not be able to give that command to someone else.

Micah takes an interest in certain school subjects like geography or science. With repetition and many extra hours of help from his assistants and his mother, he eventually retains a good amount of information about these subjects. It can be disheartening when he is unable to demonstrate his learning because he cannot express himself on tests and homework assignments. Fortunately, most of his teachers have been able to look beyond his disabilities to see that he is learning in his own way.

Micah is able to remember long, involved stories from television shows, especially cartoons. At age ten he developed an interesting way of interacting with these stories. He would draw out the scenes from the story on loose-leaf notebook paper, one page per scene. Often he would substitute pictures of himself, his sister Muriel, or other family members for the characters in the story. These drawings would consume dozens of pages. At first, his parents were delighted that Micah had found a creative outlet. Perhaps this would be the medium he would use to finally express himself in his own way to the rest of the world. His parents imagined that, with practice, Micah's thoughts could be captured on paper, refined, and edited into coherent storyboards. Pencils and reams of loose-leaf paper were kept within Micah's easy access. He was encouraged to spend time in his room drawing out his stories.

Unfortunately, his storyboards never met their potential. The drawings never progressed beyond sparse stick figures like those expected from a four- or five-year-old child. The stories, upon further inspection, were verbatim re-tellings of stories from various cartoons. When he put family members into the stories, he often put himself into the main role. Other family members would sometimes be villains or other characters that suffered cartoon-inspired violence. There were generally no words on the pages, except perhaps a title page and "The End" on the last page, so Micah was encouraged to tell the stories out loud. This exercise devolved into almost incoherent rambling, often in a high, squeaky voice. Micah deeply resented any suggestions about how to refine his stories, drawings, or narratives.

After a while it became clear that his storyboards were just another form of stimming. That is, Micah received some sort of sensory satisfaction from replaying the stories in his mind and from drawing the simple figures. In this case there was almost no creative input on his part. The drawings of family members being injured, whether malicious or not, needed to be discouraged. Over time, no development was observed in the drawings or the stories. The drawings actually became less complex. Micah was never restricted from making more storyboards; he simply stopped making them around age thirteen. The storyboards were amusing at first, but Micah's family was glad when they no longer appeared.

Micah is a child of the digital age. He has been immersed in visual images on television and computer screens ever since he was able to focus on them. This was not by design. His parents provided him with all the toys, books, and creative playthings found in almost every home with young children. He was encouraged to play outdoors, play with his sister, build and stack things, and generally explore the world around him. But all this was no match for television. After Micah developed his autistic tendencies, he was no longer able to concentrate on a toy or a game long enough to have a positive play experience. This contrasted with television, where he could watch programs for hours, sometimes with rapt attention. It was never clear why he was able to focus on television shows. Perhaps it was the constantly changing images, the flicker of the screen, or some other factor that seems to both calm and stimulate everyone who watches television.

At times, Micah's parents actually welcomed Micah's interest in television. They did not use television as a babysitter, although like every parent they took advantage of their kids' television time to catch up on tasks around the house. For Micah, watching television attentively was one of the few activities he could do like a typical child. The fact he would pay attention for extended periods of time, follow a story line, and grasp basic concepts within a television program indicated that he was not mentally challenged in all respects. His parents stocked the living room with dozens of "educational" videos. They hoped to keep both their kids away from the commercials and vapid content running through much of children's television programming. They also hoped the kids would learn some useful things during their time in front of the screen.

Micah took naturally to the computer. Although he would not read books, he would read long passages as part of a computer game. Puzzles and other tasks that presented a challenge in the real world seemed more manageable on the computer screen.

Micah learned to type at an early age. He did just fine in his "keyboarding" lessons at school. Anyone who struggled through a high school typing class years ago has to be amazed at the way elementary school kids pick up this skill so easily today. Micah's handwriting skills did not develop nearly as quickly. At age fourteen, his handwriting still looked like the handwriting of a six to eight year old. His typing skills, however, continued to improve. He typed with speed and accuracy comparable to kids his age and better than some adults, especially those of us over age sixty. He even mastered typing using a phone keypad, with all its difficult requirements.

Micah's affinity for computers and typing naturally led him to email. Like anyone, he enjoys receiving notes from other people. When they are handwritten, he seldom replies in kind. It is just too inconvenient and difficult to find the right paper and pen, compose a reply, and then struggle to write it out. Never mind the effort to address, stamp, and mail the envelope, which is usually delegated to his mom. But when Micah receives an email, he can promptly type out a reply. His spelling, sentence structure, and content still need a lot of work, but, as his parents point out, it is not too far behind the nearly incomprehensible grammatical train wrecks that other teenagers and young adults exchange.

Micah has even been known to communicate too much using electronic media, which is something of an accomplishment for a person with autism. When he was fourteen his parents purchased a cell phone for him. He seldom used it, but it was reassuring to know he had a phone for emergency calls. During a rare vacation away from his mom, Micah discovered text messaging. He sent several "texts" to his mom from his phone each day. They were all relevant messages about what he was doing or asking what she was doing. Finally, his mom had to ask that he stop sending so many texts. She was in a different time zone, and the message ring tone on her phone was keeping her awake at night. (She could not mute the phone at night for other reasons.) She hated to discourage any communication with her son, but there is always a limit.

For Micah and other people with autism, electronic communication has many advantages. First and foremost it eliminates the need to make eye contact with someone. A great deal of information is communicated through facial expression, tone of voice, and body gestures in a typical conversation. People with autism often have difficulty looking at someone else and interpreting their body language.

Furthermore, they may not have the communication skills to make their own body language jive with the words they are speaking. With electronic communications, neither party in a conversation can make use of body language, so the communications must be more basic and straightforward in order to be understood clearly. This works to the advantage of a person with autism. It can level the playing field with the other person in the conversation.

As electronic messages become faster and more common, they are becoming more of a substitute for verbal communication. For some people with autism, this will be a welcome development. Electronic verbal communications such as video conferencing, phone calls with video feeds (e.g., Skype), and interactive virtual reality (e.g., Second Life) are also becoming more available. Many autistic people find watching someone talk to them from a computer screen, even in real time, to be far easier and less stressful than looking at them directly.

WHAT GRANDPARENTS CAN DO

Grandparents need to recognize that all people communicate better in some ways than in other ways. Encourage your grandchild with autism to communicate with you as much as possible. But don't be surprised if typical channels of communication prove difficult.

You can help by teaching him and training him to use certain standard phrases that people use. For example, instead of saying, "No," at the dinner table, teach him to say, "No thank you, I don't care for carrots [or whatever else is being served]." This is generally true for all your grandchildren, but it can be extra challenging, extra important, and extra rewarding for your grandchild with autism.

When you have an opportunity to talk with your grandchild on the phone or in person, talk with them for as long as possible. They may not have conversations with people very often because of their lack of friends, communication, and social skills. You may find it difficult to create conversation if you only get one word responses to questions. It can be frustrating when you get rambling, fragmented discussions about things that seem trivial or completely foreign to you. If you are patient and persistent, you may provide them with rare opportunities to experience and practice sustained conversations. It may be easier for a child with autism to converse on the telephone since he doesn't have to deal with direct contact.

In person, try to talk to your grandchild in a manner appropriate for someone their age. It is easy to lapse into a condescending tone and assume that they do not understand what you are saying. They probably understand more than you realize, but they may need explanations of some basic vocabulary and idioms.

When a new channel of communication is discovered, utilize it to the fullest. Perhaps it will be email or pictures drawn on cards. Frequently the communications focus on some other topic that is of interest to the child. With Micah, almost any communication becomes longer and more sophisticated if Transformers or a movie is part of the exchange.

Micah's ability to converse on subjects of his interest is illustrated by the following experience. As a high school student, Micah developed an interest in history. One fall he asked, "Grandma, did you ever hear of 9/11, when airplanes flew into the towers in New York City?"

"Yes, of course I have."

"What were you doing that day?"

Since it was the tenth anniversary of the famous date, I realized they had discussed it at school. I was delighted since Micah rarely reports on anything happening at school or in his classes unless quizzed. When I expressed my pleasure to his parents, eyes rolled, and it was explained that for several days 9/11 was all Micah wanted to talk about. Still, I thought the question of what I was doing that day revealed a new dimension to his personality.

Above all, grandparents must realize that lack of communication does not always indicate lack of intelligence. Communication is critical for a child's develop fully. For children with autism, that development can take longer and may come through unusual channels.

Let's face it, many grandparents have some difficulty communicating with each of their grandchildren. It is not so surprising when you consider the generation gap and especially the cultural gap which has developed through the rapid development of modern communication techniques—specifically, computers, television, cell phones, and DVDs.

Basically, autistic children usually are reluctant to communicate with others, not just grandparents. Unless drawn out, they are happy to be in their own world, and unless they desire something for themselves they see no need to communicate. Thus, they may show little interest in Grandma and Grandpa. Beyond that, because they are reluctant to communicate, they are slow to develop communication skills. Grandparents need to develop techniques of their own which can break through these barriers. Visits to museums with displays of interest to the child can be beneficial. Be prepared for possible short attention spans.

Speech characteristics of young children are often difficult for older people, and you may find encouraging them to slow down can be helpful. The same is true with autistic children, but problems sometimes are magnified by their voice control. When they are speaking rapidly and using a high pitched voice, they can become very difficult to understand. A technique we observed in speech therapy was to tell the child to talk slowly and talk in a low big boy voice. Therapists illustrate "in a low big boy voice" by speaking slowly in a deep-toned voice.

Communicating can be a difficult chore for your grandchild and may require concentrated effort on his part. Saying, "Look at me," when in conversation and maintaining eye contact will help the child be more effective in communication.

Family pet, Samantha, learned this early on when Micah was telling her to sit and beg. He was heard to say, "Look at me Samantha." There was no biscuit for Samantha if she did not look at Micah.

The result of these efforts is a degree in patience, patience, patience.

PUBLIC PARTICIPATION

A Musical Turn Around

The musical presented every springtime by third and fourth graders is an eagerly awaited event at Withrow Elementary School. The students dramatize a story with song and dance. It is a highlight of the school year and is well attended by parents and extended family members, including grandparents.

When Micah was a third grader, Hollis and I arrived at the school and joined the crowd seated in rows on folding chairs in the combination gym, cafeteria, and auditorium. Parents and family members were sitting on the edge of their chairs, craning their necks to catch a glimpse of the smiling face of their favorite student as the children filed into the room and clattered to their spot on the risers. As students paraded in, we were not surprised Micah was not among them. We realized facing so large a crowd of people would be very difficult for him.

After all the children had taken their places, we noticed Micah being led into the room by a teacher, then seated on a small chair, not looking at the audience but facing a wall off to the side of the other third graders. We could not glimpse those blue eyes, only his back and his blond hair with a spiking cowlick. He never moved throughout the concert. Our emotions tangled together as we experienced shock, disappointment, and pity for Micah. I fought to push aside embarrassment, so as not to show chagrin or discomfort for others to witness.

How was this effecting Micah, we wondered? I felt an urge to go to him, take his hand, and lead him out of the room. I imagined hugging him in the hallway and telling him he was special and we loved him.

But I knew his teachers were caring educators who Micah's parents, seated quietly nearby, respected. Then too, I realized Micah did not have the same emotions as the other students at this point in his life. He perhaps felt no isolation and possibly perceived he was part of the program. His mom, Susan, told us he knew all the songs and was probably following along, if not audibly, at least in his mind. No one had forced him into the room, so perhaps in his own way, in his own world, he was happy. It was just Grandma and Grandpa who had to make an adjustment.

One year later, after the difficult third grade experience, there was a turn-around.

What it a thrill it was when we arrived, to see Micah handing out programs to people as they filed into the auditorium. Jackie Patrick, his para-professional aide was seated nearby giving him encouragement. Micah introduced her by saying, "Mrs. Patrick, this is my Poppa and my Grandma." A simple introduction, not a monumental achievement for a fourth grader, but it was a pleasant, wonderful surprise for us.

Then, as we sat on our folding chairs in the auditorium, a greater thrill was in store for us. Just as in the previous year, students paraded on stage without Micah. We were braced for this, but to our amazement, Micah came bounding onto the stage holding a large sign in front of his classmates, bearing the program title. He was proud of the sign because, we were informed later, he had made it himself, with considerable help. Then as he stood on the stage with a heartwarming smile, he began a program introduction, speaking rapidly, spewing words he supposedly wrote by himself. His closing remarks were, "Written by Micah, produced by Micah, and directed by Micah." With that, he jumped off the stage to an enthusiastic ovation by the audience, teachers, and classmates.

Because he spoke so rapidly, we did not understand much of what he said, but that was not important to us. We knew it was one of the finest speeches ever given. He did not participate with the other children, just ran off into the hallway to sit near the door with his para-professional. Although he knew the songs and dance steps, he could not face a crowd of people. We realized he had come far in one year, but still had miles to go.

The teachers worked hard to encourage Micah. Being touted as the assistant director was important to him, but it may have been overshadowed by the events of the previous evening at dress rehearsal. When the rehearsal concluded, his classmates lined up to give him "high fives." What a tribute to a wonderful, caring faculty! They were able to reach into his world and begin drawing Micah into theirs. They obviously had been a huge influence on his classmates, teaching them to respect him and to support him.

For many months, Micah proudly displayed his program sign in his home and listened to a DVD of the presentation, a disc complete with his picture. Sometimes in the privacy of the living room, he would sing and dance with the DVD. Hopefully, he was proud of his achievements.

DISCUSSION

It would be wonderful if we could say the sign-holding performance was proof that Micah had made a large advancement in his development and maturity. But, alas, much of his behavior in the following weeks resorted to past levels. We learned that such behavior is typical for a child with autism. Progress is often measured by two steps forward and one step back. We found behavioral improvements could temporarily disappear, and we learned not to be disappointed when that happened, realizing the improvements would likely return at a later date.

Micah's parents chose mainstreaming for him over private special needs education. That of course is an extremely personal selection to make, perhaps requiring the aid of a child psychologist, since every child with autism has varying abilities. Mainstreaming at public school has provided socialization with peers and allowed Micah to perform well in math and science. In courses more difficult for him, he received instruction in special needs classes.

An unusual stimulus, such as the excitement of an annual musical program, can spawn above-normal performance in any student. Perhaps such was the case with Micah. He had not lost the fear of facing crowds, nor shyness in claiming achievements. However, in witnessing his performance, we gained confidence in his potential capabilities, and were encouraged to continue working on his skills.

Music therapy is a popular treatment for the symptoms of autism. It can be in the form of structured therapy, or simply music education like typical children receive. Music can enrich the lives of autistic people just like anyone else, but it also can improve speech and communication skills. Music therapy sessions focus on rhythm and repetition, working common speech patterns and vocabulary into the songs performed by students. Students who are non-verbal can sometimes sing what they cannot speak.

Micah's experience with piano lessons was probably typical for many children with autism. Micah's sister Muriel began taking piano lessons with an excellent local teacher, Lynn Foster. Muriel was very musical by nature and approached her piano training with enthusiasm. Micah tagged along to the piano lessons. Ms. Foster agreed to give Micah lessons right after Muriel's lessons. It must have been a challenge to prepare lessons and change teaching styles for two students with such different abilities. She understood that Micah would need to go at a slower pace than most students and that he would respond differently to the exercises and elementary pieces she put in front of him. Recitals would be out of the question.

Micah and his mom, Susan, gamely practiced piano lessons at home. Micah actually enjoyed some of the written assignments that taught him about notes and scales. He was much better at routine exercises such as scales rather than playing songs. Micah did not seem to notice the difference. An exercise of playing scales in different keys was just as melodic as Beethoven's *Für Elise*. The lessons continued for about three years. Micah made some slow progress, but nothing dramatic. Eventually they decided to discontinue the lessons, and both mother and student felt a sense of relief.

Micah's parents were grateful to Ms. Foster for her patience with teaching Micah piano lessons. Not all teachers take on a student with autism, but many find it rewarding. Many students with autism have sensitive hearing, often with perfect pitch. Occasionally musicians with autism display unusual talent that seems to arise from their autism. They can be obsessive about repeating musical patterns and getting a passage "just right," much to the enjoyment of their audience. More often the symptoms of autism get in the way of typical musical instruction. Students become easily distracted by lights or other movement in the room. If they hear music played one way, it can be difficult for them to accept it any other way. For example, if they hear a simplified version of a song or a song played incorrectly, they may also play it that way forever and refuse to change. Loud noises, such as a band rehearsal, can be irritating to their sensitive hearing. Limitations in hand movements or other motor skills may limit the ability to play an instrument correctly. As with so much of teaching autistic children, patience and repetition are keys. With time, music can enliven an autistic child like nothing else, and even the small achievements are a joy.

WHAT GRANDPARENTS CAN DO

It is difficult to control emotions at times when dealing with a special needs grandchild. It is natural to compare those grandchildren with other children and to feel disappointment when they fall far below performances of their peers. Some may even think a poor performance on the part of a grandchild is a reflection on them, on their family, on their children. Obviously, it is important to deal with those feelings and move forward with an effort to be proud of the small achievements of a grandchild with autism.

We can hearten the child's parents, siblings, and the child with autism by being present at special events, even though we know it may be painful. Only through such participation, if distance and health permit it, can we truly understand the struggles of our children as they rear a child with autism. Our involvement can speak to others in our extended family and the community. It can say, "We all need to help this family as they strive to raise this child."

As grandparents we can show gratitude to our grandchild's teachers. Mainstreaming special needs children has added a burden on educators and all staff in those schools who are providing training on many levels for challenged children. A verbal thank you, a written note of appreciation, or, if possible, a gift to the school such as a book for the library, is a good way to show gratitude.

If you are musically inclined, share the gift of music with your grandchild. It can be anything from singing songs with them or teaching them simple tunes on the piano. Remember that patience and repetition are required before some musical skills blossom. Gifts of music albums can be useful too. Be certain to check which medium the child and his family use and prefer (CDs, MP3 downloads, etc.). Being familiar with current music is one way a child with autism can relate to his peers and the popular culture around him.

Grandparent participation from near or far can be thrilling. News of small advancements mean much and is wonderful to share with family and friends.

CELEBRATIONS AND EVENTS

Micah's Birthday Party

"What day is Micah's birthday party?" This question was addressed to Micah's mom, Susan, when she picked him up from school one day when he was a fourth grader.

"What party? Did Micah tell you he is having a birthday party?" she asked, surprise and excitement rising in her.

"Yes, he did, but he didn't tell us what day, or time, or anything like that," said Sammy, a serious young fellow with bangs hanging nearly over his eyes. He frequently attempted to befriend Micah, but usually received no response.

"Well, Sammy, I will call your mother tonight with the details."

This was an exciting breakthrough for Micah's family. Most children anticipate and enjoy the attention they receive on their birthdays. This was not so for Micah. Over the years, on his special day he did not want any attention directed toward him and would retreat when grandparents or other relatives tried any sort of celebration. Presents were meaningless to him, and he would pay no heed to his birthday cake. His sister, Muriel, or a special cousin would blow the candles for him. Singing the birthday song caused him to cover his ears, look away, and possibly leave the room. "Don't sing. Don't sing," he would plead.

A change began when Micah was an eight-year-old third grader. Some thoughtful parents of his classmates would invite him to join parties for their children. Of course his mom or dad had to accompany him at all times. He appeared oblivious to the games and fun surrounding him, but perhaps he was observing in his own way, from his own world, learning about parties.

As his ninth birthday approached, he continued to accept the idea of a party. That week he began counting the days until the party, one of those precious indications that Micah was slowly coming out of his cocoon into our world. On the day of the party he awoke and announced, "This is the best day of my young life!" He may not have understood the full meaning of this proclamation. Perhaps he heard the phrase on television or from another child. However, he was using it correctly for this occasion.

The party took place at a game arcade with a generally low noise level. A miniature golf course was adjacent to the facility. The arcade had a good-sized table where everyone could gather for snacks and cake. Three or four friends, selected with the help of Micah's teacher, three cousins, an aunt, sister Muriel, his parents, and his grandfather and I rounded out the guest participants.

The game arcade offered games which rewarded players with tickets they could redeem for toys and trinkets. Varying numbers of tickets were awarded by the game machines. Micah reacted differently to the games than other children at the party.

"Look, I got twenty tickets from one machine," a guest would yell. While his friends, sister, and cousins ran to the machines producing the most tickets, Micah played one machine repeatedly. He was satisfied to collect one or two tickets over and over again. Rewards were of little interest to him, and he appeared oblivious to the activity of his friends.

Micah did enjoy the air hockey game, even though it put him in direct competition with a friend. He was not disturbed when he was losing, nor was he elated when winning. He was content with just hitting the puck back and forth.

Miniature golf was of great interest to Micah. He enjoyed going through the sequence of numbered holes, announcing the number as he arrived at the starting point of each hole. He hit the ball, chased it, and hit it again, not taking aim, but sending it in the general direction of the hole. The number of strokes meant nothing to him; he was just having fun. He was delighted when the ball disappeared into one of the underground tubes and magically appeared somewhere else. He was intent on completing the series of holes quickly. He did not play golf with other children, only with his grandfather.

During Micah's special day, we observed him developing some social skills such as enjoying, not objecting, to being part of a group of people. He did enjoy opening some gifts. As a toddler he often refused to open gifts for his birthdays.

It is unpredictable how kids will treat their peers who have disabilities such as autism. They can be mean and hurtful, but they also can be extraordinarily kind. When the birthday cake appeared at the party, Micah's parents cautioned everyone not to sing the birthday song, as Micah was very sensitive to singing. One of his friends spoke up and said, "Hey, remember at school when we were learning sign language? We did the birthday song!"

The candles were lit, and Micah and adult guests watched as his friends quietly signed words to the birthday song, as best they could remember. Micah watched, but he could still not overcome his shyness enough to blow out the candles, so his friends did it for him.

Later that week, we had another small birthday party for Micah, again with a cake and candles, but no singing. This time he was able to blow out the candles by himself. We were thankful for this and other small advancements in social integration, which are often taken for granted in children without autism.

DISCUSSION

The following observations by this grandmother concerning the behavior of children with autism must be read with the reminder that autistic children are varied but often have some characteristics in common.

The birthday party was one of the few times Micah ever participated in a sports activity not highly organized by adults. This is typical of children and teens with autism. Even in a structured environment, team sports can be overwhelming to people with autism. The reasons behind their difficulty are easy to understand when you consider the nature of autism. Team sports have been described as our highest expression of social skills. They first require organization of the participants into teams. Often there is an authority figure, a coach, who must be respected and obeyed. Different individual assignments are given to each player, presumably based on their particular talents and strengths. During play, each team member must coordinate their movements with other team members. This requires an unspoken understanding, perception, or anticipation of what your team members are about to do. Furthermore, you must anticipate what your opponent is thinking and doing, he or she may try to make this more difficult with fake moves or even intimidation. All of this social interaction happens as fast as the players are capable of creating it. And, by the way, it must be done in coordination with complex muscle movements, often when the players are fatigued and near their physical limit.

Clearly, people with autism are unlikely to excel at team sports, almost by definition. The social skills that are repressed in autism are the same social skills necessary to participate, compete, and win in team sports. The football field, basketball court, softball diamond, etc., are places where anyone with mind-blindness or communication challenges will have difficulties. Add to this the sensory overload from loud voices, cheering audiences, and bright lights, and it is no wonder that participation in team sports may be unenjoyable or even repulsive for people with autism.

The challenges of team sports may apply even to sports in an adaptive setting. Micah is fortunate to live in an area with an active Special Olympics organization and other adaptive sports programs. For several years he was signed up to play in an adaptive T-ball league.

The league was designed for children and teens with the physical and mental challenges to play baseball to the best of their abilities. The rules were set up like most T-ball leagues. Everyone gets to bat every time their team is up. The ball is placed on a tee at home plate. Each player gets as many swings as necessary to hit the ball, and can even have some coaching or assistance if necessary. Outs are seldom recorded because few players have the necessary skills to field the ball and throw it to another player. Players run around the bases until they decide to stop or until they cross home plate—whichever comes first. The score becomes rather unimportant.

The T-ball league was the highlight of the week for many players. They would put on their matching uniforms and hats and eagerly show up early for the game. The parents and coaches would help them with a variety of warm-up exercises and skills practice. When it was their turn to bat, some would go through elaborate rituals before addressing the ball. As the ball flew from the tee and they ran toward first base, squeals of excitement could be heard from the players, while cheering and shouts of encouragement erupted from parents and coaches of both teams.

For Micah, this whole scene had no appeal. He would reluctantly put on his uniform and go to the games. As soon as he arrived, he would head for a playground that was some distance from the baseball field where he could play quietly by himself. When the game started, his parents or grandparents would coax him back to the field, and he would take a seat on the end of the dugout bench. He dreaded his turn to bat, often refusing to participate. Eventually Grandpa convinced him to have a try. Micah and Grandpa swung the bat together. Grandpa held Micah's right hand as he guided him toward first base. Micah used his left hand to cover his ears to muffle the shouting. In later games, a "no cheering" rule was put into effect during Micah's at-bats. This whole scene played out again and again in silence, so as not to irritate Micah's sensitive hearing. After the game, Micah would exchange the customary high-fives with the other team, then quickly retreat to the playground to be by himself.

Micah and his family gamely participated in the T-ball league for several years. Micah never did get over his shyness and inability to enjoy or really participate in the games. A photographer from the local paper showed up one day and later published a photo of Micah running the bases with his Grandpa. Eventually the family decided to stop attending the games. Another autistic boy would climb a nearby tree and usually refuse to come down until the game was over. In general, children with autism did not respond as well to T-ball as other youngsters with special needs.

Micah later learned to enjoy other individual sporting activities like bowling, golf, and skiing, but he never wanted to participate in team sports, even in an adaptive setting. Micah and his father ski in the winter with the Lumberjacks, the local Special Olympics team. The team sets up novice, intermediate, and expert race courses on different ski slopes. Coaches teach the athletes to ski and help them improve their technique. The athletes are timed, and awards are presented at regional and state competitions. Micah has no interest in racing, so he and his father usually ski on other slopes, which is fun for them and just fine with the Special Olympics organizers. They have noticed that while most of the athletes with Down's Syndrome and other intellectual issues enjoy the challenge and competition of the race courses, many of the athletes with autism prefer to ski other runs at their own pace.

For many years, into his teen years, Micah has had little concept of friends. His extreme shyness is certainly a major deterrent to making friends, but he also seems to have no sense of the fact that he has few friends. This may be a blessing until such age that he enjoys friendships. Hurt feelings or disappointment at not being included are not part of his cognizance.

Fortunately for Micah, he has cousins accepting of his behavior. They formed a healthy relationship during day care, provided since babyhood by Micah's aunt, Wendy Baxter, near St. Paul, Minnesota.

Workshops and skill training for making friends is offered by the Autism Society of Minnesota. Other state and city autism societies may offer the same opportunity, as well as organizations such as Courage Center.

WHAT GRANDPARENTS CAN DO

At a birthday party with family or with other children, gathering around a table for a game of Old Maid, Hearts, or Scrabble can be so much fun, but the festivity may be dampened when an autistic grandchild refuses to participate. In such instances, one grandparent or other family member can withdraw to read a book, play a game, or watch a DVD with the autistic child. Playing a game on Wii is a good choice. It may be wise to do this individual activity near where the game or group activity is taking place, so as not to reinforce the desire for isolation by the child with autism.

As at Micah's party, the child with autism may want to do activities other children are doing, but not with them. The child may consent to do an activity with a grandparent or other adult. This frees parents to keep the party going for the guests. It is also an opportunity for a grandparent to keep the autistic child near the center of activity while trying to engage him or her with other children.

Everyone who cares for someone with mental and/or emotional disabilities should be aware of Special Olympics. Their local and national websites are easy to find. This wonderful organization provides excellent activities that are usually, but not always, centered around sporting activities. In addition, they provide training and other assistance to people who work and play with handicapped individuals. Grandparents can not only find out about programs in their area, they can also participate as coaches.

A grandparent can love and enjoy an autistic grandchild as they are. The challenge is not comparing them to children with no autism and to rejoice at the small improvements they make socially and with new skills. Autistic children can seem happy within their own world at the same time that we try to pull them into ours.

ALLERGIES, IMMUNIZATIONS, AND SPECIAL DIETS

Micah Is Sick Again

The phone call from the school nurse's office put an abrupt end to Micah's parents' scheduled plans for the day. "Hello, Mrs. Grubb? Micah is in my office, and he seems to have those hives again. I think he should go home." Every parent dreads those phone calls, but they are part of the parenting experience—except that this was the third one that week.

When Micah's mom arrived at the school, she found a happy and bouncy third grader in the nurse's office. Micah did not look sick at all, but she took him home anyway as a precaution. He had been very ill a few days earlier, so he was kept home from school. A trip to the doctor's Urgent Care office confirmed that Micah did not have strep throat or an ear infection. His high temperature and upset stomach responded well to rest, Tylenol, and television, so he went back to school the next day. But each of the following two days he ended up in the nurse's office and was sent home.

What could be causing the illness? Micah was not faking it. He had conjured up imaginary illnesses before, but it would take real talent for a little kid to give himself hives at will. The school was aware of his allergies to apples, soy, and milk, and they were very careful to avoid those things.

Micah's mom talked to his teachers. "What was he doing before he got sick?" she asked.

"Come to think of it, the hives seemed to appear around the time we have our snack," his teacher remembered. "But we only had some crackers and some cranberry/raspberry juice, so he should be OK with those. But I'll check the ingredients."

To everyone's surprise, the main ingredient in cranberry/raspberry juice is apple juice. The mystery was solved. A different drink was served with the snacks, and the hives did not reappear.

Micah's parents could not get upset with the school teachers. They were generally very conscientious about allergy problems. Micah's parents had made their share of missteps, too. As Micah grows older, he has learned to police his own food for known allergens. This is good, but it only adds to his many anxieties about trying new foods.

DISCUSSION

The following discussion is in no way a comprehensive discussion of allergies, immunizations, and special diets. It is merely background information that should lead to further research by families and to discussions with the child's doctor. Here it must be emphasized again that all children with autism are different, so extreme care must be taken to tailor treatment to best suit each child. Micah's parents have researched this topic carefully and have held many discussions with physicians. I have borrowed insights from their investigations.

Doctors and researchers generally agree that autism is somehow related to problems with the immune system. A high correlation exists between the incidence of autism in children and the incidence of immune system problems such as allergies, infections, and poor food digestion. A great deal of scientific research is focused on identifying and understanding how immune system problems interact with autism and/or vice versa.

Children with autism are susceptible to common allergies (dust, pollen, nuts, bee stings, etc.) just like other children. The allergens that cause the reaction will vary from person to person. Allergic reactions will often change and become more or less severe as a child grows up.

Many books and websites tout that a child's autism can be dramatically improved or cured by identifying and eliminating allergens from the child's diet and environment. You may wish to be skeptical of these claims. They are usually found to be rooted in a few anecdotal cases or limited scientific studies. Broader, well-designed studies seldom, if ever, support the results of the smaller studies. Certainly, allergic reactions need to be avoided for other health reasons but doing so is practically impossible, and avoiding allergens completely probably will not "cure" autism.

Childhood immunizations have attracted great attention and concern as a potential cause of autism. Consequently, some parents have withheld common vaccinations from their children for fear of inducing autism. Other parents are left to wonder if they unknowingly caused their child's disease simply by following their doctor's advice.

The concern over immunizations and autism is easily understood. As already noted, there is a relationship between autism and problems with the immune system. Symptoms of autism often begin to appear between the ages of one and three. This is the same time that most children receive vaccinations that cause significant changes in the body's immune system.

Some doctors have suggested that thimerosal, a preservative containing mercury used in vaccines, triggered autism. Although no definite relationship was identified, the medical community is actively working to find alternatives and remove thimerosal and mercury from all vaccines.

A massive research effort is currently underway, so new and better information about immunizations will be coming out for the next several years. Even if childhood immunizations are found to be linked to autism, the risk of immunizing needs to be weighed against the well-documented risk of not immunizing against other terrible diseases. This is such a hot topic within the autism community that grandparents should be aware of it, perhaps draw their own conclusions, but not impose those conclusions on the autistic child's family.

Various drugs can be used to treat the physical disorders frequently afflicting those with autism. Not all doctors or parents treat children with drugs the same way. Common drugs include laxatives, allergy medications (antihistamines), attention deficit drugs, and antidepressants.

It is easy to find testimonials from parents and doctors that tell the story of how a child's autism was improved or cured after adding or eliminating certain foods from his diet. The testimonials are likely genuine. But if you look closely, you will see they generally reflect the experience of one family or a select group of families. When special diets are tested in broad, well-designed scientific studies, the results are not nearly so promising.

One of the more common special diets is the gluten-free casein-free (GFCF) diet. Casein is found mostly in dairy products. Gluten is a part of wheat and several other grains. When any food is digested it releases chemicals into the blood stream. Casein and gluten become peptides that act as opiates as they circulate through the body. They can cause behavior changes and problems with digestion. The theory is that children with autism are more susceptible to these effects than other children and that removing gluten and/or casein from the diet may reduce or eliminate the symptoms in some children.

Limiting a child's diet can have unintentional detrimental consequences. Radical diet changes or restrictions should be done only under the supervision of a physician. The risks of special diets include malnutrition and new and different behavioral problems. Special diets can cause difficulties and stress for the parents and families. Special diets and food supplements may also be a financial burden.

Why does one child respond so positively to simple changes in diet, while another child seems to be locked into a recurring pattern of autistic behavior? If we only knew the answer! Autism is often compared to a puzzle with many unique pieces that do not seem to fit together. We can only examine each piece individually, try to understand how it compares to the other pieces, and seek to fit it into the larger puzzle as a whole. Eventually, through research, enough pieces will fit together, enabling someone to step back and recognize the picture they create.

WHAT GRANDPARENTS CAN DO

It is important for grandparents to adhere to wishes of parents of a child. Grandparents should become involved in visits to the doctor or other diagnostic pursuits only if parents request it.

Grandparents need to be aware of the grandchild's dietary restrictions. This is true of any grandchild, but it may be especially important for your grandchild with autism. Be sure to check with parents from time to time to ask if anything has changed. Maybe a new allergy has been recognized or the child no longer reacts to a food that was previously off-limits.

Special diets should be followed strictly. A visit to Grandma's house is not a reason to have a "treat" of restricted foods. For example, if your grandchild is on a casein-free diet, do not allow them to have a little bit of cheese as a snack. Even small amounts of restricted foods can interfere with the intended benefits of a special diet.

The topic of immunizations is sensitive and difficult for all families, particularly those with a history of autism. You will need to decide whether your interest and input on decisions regarding immunizations would be welcome by your grandchild's parents or not. This is usually a private decision made by parents with advice of their doctor and other trusted advisors. If you do offer your input, be sure you first do homework on risks and benefits of childhood immunizations. Do not take your information from only one source and present it to the parents as being authoritative. There are many different opinions out there, and new and better data and information are becoming available all the time.

Most grandparents are very familiar with drugs and prescriptions. Of course, it is always a good idea to have a current supply of first aid supplies and common drugs (Benadryl for allergies, children's pain relievers, etc.) on hand, but to be given out only with a parent's permission. You will also need to know if your grandchild needs prescription medications, especially if you are watching them for more than a few hours. A detailed, written list of instructions from the parents is critical.

Be aware, many online sources and shopping mall nutritional stores advertise expensive supplements promising a cure for autism or improvements in symptoms. None of them have proved to be an effective "cure" for autism. Do not be critical of your grandchild's parents if they have not exposed their child to the latest treatments advertised on the internet and elsewhere. There are many reasons to be cautious and skeptical about starting new treatments. Similarly, do not send every magazine article or stray piece of information to the parents to suggest a cure for autism is close at hand. You and the parents should research different therapies closely so you fully understand the potential benefits and risks.

All of this is scary and serious stuff, but it should not stop you from spending time with your grandchildren. Even when you are away from the rest of the family, the chance of anything really dangerous arising is not much greater than with typical grandchildren. If something does go wrong, parents and emergency services are just a cell phone call away. The much greater risk is that your grandchild (and you) could miss out on all the fun and developmental growth that can come from the grandparent–grandchild relationship.

FOOD FAVORITES AND AVERSIONS

Micah Tries Krabby Patties

Micah loves Krabby Patties, sort of. When he indicated that he might like to try this new food item, Micah's parents jumped at the opportunity to introduce some more variety into his diet. At age twelve he had insisted on meal fare which consisted almost exclusively of French fries, plain spaghetti, cheese pizza, and sometimes chicken nuggets. With great cajoling, raw pears, grapes, and peas could be added. Autistic children are notoriously picky eaters. Sensory issues and complex social situations can combine to make meal times difficult on both autistic children and the people dining with them.

To understand the allure of Krabby Patties, you must first know the back story of SpongeBob SquarePants. Micah is a huge fan of SpongeBob. Fortunately for Micah's family, SpongeBob is one of those rare children's cartoons that has some humor and appeal for adults as well. SpongeBob works as a fry cook at the Krusty Krab, the local greasy spoon hamburger joint in his home town of Bikini Bottom. The signature item on the menu is the irresistibly delicious Krabby Patty.

The evil Plankton owns a rival restaurant, the Chum Bucket. Many SpongeBob episodes focus on Plankton's diabolical plots to steal the Krabby Patty secret recipe. Micah laughs hysterically when Plankton's plans are inevitably foiled.

In one SpongeBob episode, the Krabby Patty secret recipe is finally revealed to the viewers (but not to Plankton). The narrator dramatically and slowly announces the ingredients: A sesame seed bun! A hamburger patty! Ketchup! Mustard! Lettuce! Onions! Three pickle slices! At this point, Micah was beside himself with excitement. Now he knew the secret recipe! Even better, this looked like something he could make!

Hamburgers were not on Micah's short list of foods he would eat at age twelve. "Mom!" he exclaimed. "I could make a Krabby Patty for dinner some time!" His mother was excited too, to add a new food to Micah's food list. She was determined to make the most of it. She studied the cartoon DVD and bought buns and pickle slices identical to the ones in the show. She carefully fried a flat hamburger patty, being careful not to undercook or overcook it, thereby adding unnecessary marks or colors.

The ingredients were carefully laid out on the dining room table. Micah gleefully assembled them, announcing each one to the family. Everyone collectively held their breath as Micah took the finished Krabby Patty in two hands and raised it to his mouth. He paused, then took a wee nibble from the bottom part of the bun. He tried again, opening his mouth and putting the hamburger close to his lips. Then he put the Krabby Patty down and quickly left the room.

"Wait! Where are you going? You should at least try one bite," his mother yelled after him.

"I can't," was Micah's only reply. No amount of coaxing or encouragement could make him change his mind. The rest of the family made their own versions of the Krabby Patty and ate them, although somewhat dejectedly. The burgers were not quite as good as touted in the cartoons, and it was sad to think that Micah could not enjoy something he had anticipated so eagerly.

DISCUSSION

Typical kids have food aversions. They tend to like sweet, processed, familiar foods, and they reject some highly nutritious foods like vegetables. Some of the differences between a child's preferences and an adult's preferences is likely due to the changing and maturing of taste buds and other sensors as the child grows up. Another factor is developing familiarity with different types of food.

Actually, most adults have food aversions too, but they probably do not confront them every day. People in foreign countries eat many foods that seem repulsive to us. In the United States, few people would consider sitting down to eat a bowl of termites. Yet in some African countries, eating termites is a delicious and nutritious treat. Even familiar foods can be difficult to enjoy in another country where the flavor or texture of the food is just a little bit different.

For an autistic child, the typical challenge of eating some "grown-up" foods is complicated by unusual sensitivities related to autism. Autistic children often react oddly to certain textures or other stimulation. Crunchy, creamy, sweet, salty, and other sensations are usually associated with food in a positive way. To a person with autism, they can be extremely unpleasant. We can only imagine what it must feel like to them to encounter strange tastes or textures. Facing a bowl of unfamiliar breakfast cereal may seem like facing a bowl of termites to some people.

Overcoming resistance to eating a balanced, healthful diet is one of the key challenges in raising an autistic child. The classic techniques used by most parents to encourage good eating habits are the starting point. These include making the food as appealing as possible and serving small portions. Some system of reward and punishment is often involved as well (i.e., "No dessert until you finish your peas"). Autistic children with developmental delays may require this type of behavior modification far longer than typical children.

The other side of this coin is overeating a single type of food. Typical children will sometimes eat a favorite food until it makes them sick. Children with autism are not immune to this behavior. Micah's parents have met many autistic children who, for some unknown reason, crave French fries. They can eat an enormous amount and still look for more. Obviously, this behavior needs to be monitored and restricted.

For extreme cases of food aversion, professional help is available. A professional therapist will often work on overcoming the aversions by using de-sensitizing techniques. In Micah's case, he would not eat any type of new food. A therapist introduced him to a six-step process that helps Micah get past the initial aversion. First, Micah picks up the food with his hands or on a fork or spoon. Next, he touches the food to his lips. He then gives the food a lick. Then he "hides" the food in his mouth without chewing or swallowing. The next step is a small bite, followed by bigger bites, chewing, and swallowing. Not all the steps have to come in one sitting, and sometimes the early steps need to be repeated over several meal times.

Dealing with an autistic child's food aversions can lead to some bizarre parenting moments. Micah's parents never imagined that they would have to pay good money to a professional to convince their kid to eat cheese doodles. On the positive side, Micah will not eat candy, drink soda pop, or consume most other sweet things, so they have been spared many of the typical struggles to limit those foods. His parents often catch themselves saying things that no "good" parent would ever say, like, "You're not leaving the table until you try some ice cream. Then you can have more grapes."

Table manners are not easy. Everyone needs to be taught good manners. They take many years to learn and a lifetime to master. With autistic children, the development of table manners is usually impeded in the same way that other learning and social skills are delayed. Unfortunately, this can require a lot of patience on the part of those teaching the skills as well as everyone else at the table.

Sensory issues can lead to bad manners as well. In recent years Micah has developed the ability to continually bite a hot dog until the entire hot dog and bun are in his mouth. It is easy to laugh at this stunt until you realize that it was unintentional. It leaves him unable to swallow and in some discomfort. He apparently lacks the sensory inputs that tell most people to stop putting food in their mouth temporarily so they can chew and swallow.

Restaurants present autistic people with a whole slate of challenges and difficulties. They have to enter a building that may be new to them and is filled with strangers. They need to read and comprehend information from the menu, then make a decision. Micah would not look at a waiter or waitress, nor would he order his own food until he was thirteen or fourteen. Often he would slouch down in his seat as if to hide when it was time to order food.

The restaurant may be loud, with people moving fast and chaotically around the table. It can be very difficult for autistic children to interact appropriately with the people at their table and occasionally with people at other tables. Then there are all the issues related to eating food politely. As they grow older, they need to manage their money and leave a tip. Is it any wonder adult autistic people often need training to perform such a complex social activity as eating out?

The experience of eating at a restaurant can be rather challenging for the family of a child with autism. All of the issues regarding food allergies, food aversions, and table manners are still there, and now they are heightened by the presence of a lot of people you may or may not know.

For better or worse, the wait staff will be a significant factor in the enjoyment of your dining experience. Some people have the patience and understanding to put up with the strange speech or odd behavior of people with autism, and some do not. In an effort to encourage patience in waiters and waitresses, Micah's parents inform the hostess or manager of the special skill they experienced in some employees and acknowledge that skill with a special thank you tip.

Micah's mom and dad sometimes change their routine at restaurants depending on the wait staff involved. They prefer to have Micah order for himself so he can practice and develop those social skills. However, if the restaurant is crowded and the waiter or waitress seems impatient, they will order for him. The additional stress of repeating orders and potentially getting the wrong food quickly negates any potential benefit of having him order for himself. When the waiter or waitress seems more mature, patient, and relaxed, Micah orders for himself with encouragement and coaching on how it is done.

WHAT GRANDPARENTS CAN DO

Realistically, grandparents are probably not going to change a child's eating habits very much. If you are in charge of all your grandchild's meals for a prolonged time (say, more than a week), then perhaps you can use some discipline and training to encourage an improvement in diet or table manners. If you only eat meals with your grandchild occasionally, then any strict discipline is more likely to foster resistance or resentment and make meals unpleasant for everyone.

I am not suggesting that you let your autistic grandchild run wild at mealtimes, at home or in a restaurant. We should always expect children to exhibit good behavior at the table, at least as far as they are able. This includes:

- Handling food and using silverware as best they can;
- Making appropriate comments and conversation;
- Chewing and swallowing discretely;
- Politely refusing food they do not like;
- Assisting with food preparation, table setting, and cleanup when asked.

It is reasonable to expect children with autism can make progress toward eating meals with the family the same way other children can. You just need the patience and understanding that developmental delays related to autism may extend to mealtimes and eating habits. An autistic child may behave like a much younger child at the table. Unusual aversions or attractions to certain foods may be a symptom of their autism. Sorting out which behaviors are attributed to autism and which ones are just an ordinary kid's bad behaviors is probably not important in the context of grandparenting, but it is beneficial to understand there may be some overlap.

Much bad behavior takes the form of inappropriate speech, noises, or activities at the table. Hopefully, you can develop "the look" or a gentle touch that tells your grandchild to stop what they are doing, rather than continually scolding them and disrupting everyone's meal. Teach them to leave the table politely when they can no longer sit still. Consider quiet dining to be a goal. Witty conversation and proper handling of the fish fork can wait until later.

Restaurants may require some advance planning. As with any grandchild, select restaurants that are kid-friendly and family-friendly. They need to have a kids' menu or at least something on the menu that your grandchild is likely to eat. It is helpful to know ahead of time what foods your grandchild will and will not eat so you can help him order. Micah's parents actually trained him to eat those processed, deep-fried chicken pieces. They appear on almost every menu, and often they are the only things that appeal to him. Consequently, Micah has eaten an infinite variety of chicken nuggets, chicken fingers, and chicken strips in restaurants from coast to coast, usually with French fries. His parents feed him other things whenever possible, reserving the "chicken nuggets and fries" meal for those occasions when nothing else is palatable.

Good restaurants will accommodate a special order for an autistic child, but be prepared to be resourceful. You may want to look at the menu before being seated. If there is nothing that will appeal to your grandchild, ask if they will do a special order. You may need to ask a manager rather than the wait staff. If you are already seated, you may want to step away from the table to negotiate a special order with the manager, so as not to direct uncomfortable attention from others toward everyone at the table. Be prepared to pay a little extra for the service. For example, you may request to have spaghetti served without the sauce or without a vegetable on the plate, but you can still expect to pay full price. When Micah became obviously too old to order from the kids menu, we could often negotiate a "double order" of chicken nuggets and fries at double the price.

If a child has a meltdown or emotional crisis, it is often best for one grandparent to leave the restaurant with him until calm is restored.

When going to restaurants or preparing for a special meal at home, it is often helpful to inform your grandchild about what is going to happen ahead of time. Tell him what kind of restaurant it is, what is on the menu, and why you are going there. At home, tell him who will be at the table, what will be served, and information such as where everyone will be sitting. Coaching and even practice ahead of time can help an autistic child perform a difficult task. For example, help him rehearse what he will say to the waitress when ordering.

If your grandchild has a good eating experience with you, in your house or in a restaurant, try to repeat it. If they like a particular food you prepare (assuming it is a part of a healthful diet), serve it again another time. Kids will sometimes eat things at Grandma's house they would not touch at home. Similarly, some foods at certain restaurants have an unexplained appeal that simply does not transfer to other restaurants or other varieties of the same food. This can be a real bonding opportunity in the relationship with your grandchild. Everyone probably has a fond memory of Grandma's cookies (or meatloaf, spaghetti, pickles, etc.) or a favorite menu item at a local restaurant. You can foster those memories for your grandchild and help expand his eating horizons.

Remember, other parts of the eating experience can affect your grandchild as well. A favorite plate, spoon, chair, or place at the table might make them more comfortable and therefore more likely to eat a healthy meal.

'As Micah's grandparents, it is easier to boil some spaghetti or bake a frozen cheese pizza for the one or two meals he may have at our home, than try to introduce foods new to his palate. At sixteen, there are more and more foods he will eat, and his parents inform us when a new item has been added to the list.

THERAPEUTIC ACTIVITIES

Micah Meets Sam

"I won't ride a horse, I won't. I won't ride a horse," Micah repeated as he paced back and forth on the kitchen floor, shaking his hands. He was being verbally prepared for attending a horse riding camp next day. Since his parents would both be working, his grandfather and I willingly volunteered to escort him for a week of camp. Sponsored by The Autism Society of Minnesota, Camp Wahoda is located nearby in beautiful Wisconsin farm country.

The program began with five autistic boys varying in age from seven to eleven, with disparate degrees of abilities and attention spans. All were struggling over a craft project in a small room of a building near the horse barn. Some children would not sit on chairs, but walked around the table flapping their hands while others rocked back and forth in their chairs. Five camp counselors patiently worked with them, uttering words of encouragement. Eventually, five butterflies emerged from a confusion of construction paper, pipe cleaners, and glue. The camp counselors expressed pride in the accomplishments and praised the boys, who displayed little satisfaction for their work.

After a snack we left air conditioned comfort and stepped into intense July heat to tour a large vegetable garden nearby and a fenced area with a number of chickens squawking, eating, and strutting around the yard. Soon it was time to proceed to the horse stable. "I will not ride a horse," Micah chanted over and over as Grandpa carried a stiffening, struggling seven year old to the barn. Inside we met a teenage girl with soft brown eyes, wearing scuffed boots and well-worn blue jeans.

"Hi, Micah. I'm Tanya. This is Sam. He wants to be your friend. Want to stroke his soft neck?"

"No. No!" was the response. Micah peeked at Sam over his shoulder for some time before Grandpa finally lowered him onto the deep golden straw surrounding the horse. Tanya took Micah's hand and led him forward to a spot near Sam's head. She put her hand over his and slowly began stroking the chestnut mane and neck. She released her hold on Micah's hand, and he continued stroking with his fingers held rigidly. The corners of his mouth had a slight curl, the beginning of a smile. As if perceiving shyness, Sam turned his head to nudge Micah's shoulder. It the midst of musty smelling barn heat, I felt a chill run up my spine as stroking and nuzzling continued for a long while.

"Would you like to sit on Sam's back?" Tanya finally asked in a quiet voice.

"No."

"O.K. Sam needs to eat some oats; would you like to help hold this basket to his mouth?" Together they fed Sam, while silently two anxious grandparents watched.

Next day the campers struggled to make paper flowers, then visited the vegetable garden and chickens on the way to the horse barn. Micah walked hesitantly, holding Grandpa's hand. Entering Sam's stall, Micah walked up and began petting his glossy coat. "Hi, Sam," he said quietly.

After some coaxing, refusals, and more coaxing, Tanya and Grandpa lifted Micah onto Sam's back. "Now, I will lead Sam around, and your grandpa can walk beside you."

"No, stay here. Stay here. Don't move!" And stay they did, for a long time, while Tanya murmured encouraging words to boy and horse. Micah allowed no movement of Sam whatsoever during the remainder of that hour. Micah, Tanya, Sam, and grandparents all waited. We wondered what tomorrow would bring.

Day three of camp produced a change. Micah sat on Sam's back, held the reins, and smiled broadly as Tanya led them around the ring, a proud Grandpa walking along side. From the sidelines, Grandma was snapping pictures and marveling at Tanya's skill and ability to work with a child with autism.

Micah's love affair with Sam developed in the remaining days of that week. After craft time, he ran ahead of Grandpa to the barn and into Sam's stall. "Hi, Sam," he called out. "I'll ride Sam now," he told Tanya. Slowly, horse, rider, leader, and grandpa circled the riding ring, both smiling and telling Micah how proud they were of his riding abilities. That was the beginning of Micah's therapeutic relationship with horses.

Micah's horseback riding accomplishments continued beyond Sam and Camp Wahoda. The following year his parents applied for him to join River Valley Riders, a volunteer organization that sponsors therapeutic horseback riding for children and teens with disabilities in the area around St. Paul, Minnesota, and western Wisconsin. They provide services at three locations. There are other therapeutic horseback riding organizations in the area as well. Still, there is a waiting list to join.

Micah's name eventually rose to the top of the waiting list, and he was able to join the River Valley Riders group on a Wednesday evening. Micah's mom drove him to the horse arena at the county fairgrounds. Five or six horses stood tied to the white rail fence around the arena. The volunteer helpers were moving about, getting ready for the evening's activities. Some were saddling horses and moving equipment into the arena. Others were doing registration paperwork or getting snacks ready for later. Still others were standing around socializing, waiting for instructions on what to do next.

Micah was not able to get out of the car. He was paralyzed with fear over the horses and the small crowd of strangers buzzing around them. Susan sighed and went to explain the situation to the horseback riding instructors.

Susan and the instructors knew what to do. They began the process of desensitizing Micah to the surrounding environment. "How about if you just get out of the car and look at the horses?" Susan suggested.

"O.K. Well, all right."

"How about if we go stand next to one of the horses?" she asked. Micah was hesitant, but allowed Susan to take his hand and lead him toward the horses. Micah covered his ears and looked away as best he could.

One of the volunteers introduced Micah to a small, gray horse named Boss. Like all the horses, Boss was getting along in years and was very gentle and patient. Boss was standing next to a ramp used to elevate the riders so they can mount the horses more easily. "Can you pat Boss and say 'hi'?" the volunteer asked Micah. Micah let go of his mom's hand and tentatively reached toward the horse's hindquarters, patting with rigid fingers. Micah's right hand remained firmly over one ear, and he shrugged his left shoulder in attempt to cover the other ear.

At this point, Micah's mom got called away to deal with a registration issue. After a few minutes she looked back and saw, to her amazement, Micah sitting on Boss's back. Micah was not exactly smiling, and he only remained there for a few short minutes. That was enough for one day.

The next week Micah and his mom again drove to the fairgrounds. This time Micah got out of the car without urging from Susan, and one of the volunteers greeted him. She led him over to where Boss was standing. Soon Micah was wearing a riding helmet (How did she get him to do that?) and sitting on Boss's back.

Three volunteers walked Boss and Micah to the riding arena. One volunteer led Boss while the other two "side walkers" made sure Micah stayed upright in the saddle. They walked around the ring a few times and then joined a group of horses and riders at the center of the ring for a simple game.

Boss and Micah became fast friends. Micah brought home one of Boss's old horseshoes that Boss had "given" to Micah to hang in his bedroom. Micah was encouraged to give Boss one of his old shoes, for Boss's stable, but he never did. Over time Micah outgrew Boss, his legs extending down past his belly and threatening to reach the ground. Boss eventually retired and moved on to greener pastures.

Micah has continued to ride with River Valley Riders, and his grandfather has volunteered there from time to time. Micah has grown more confident in his riding. He no longer requires side walkers, and is able to talk and laugh with the volunteers as he rides. He has also improved verbal skills through conversation with leaders and side walkers.

At River Valley Riders with friend Neal, who later became a bowling companion.

While Micah has obviously benefited from therapeutic horseback riding, his family has gained as well. Two years after Micah started horseback riding, Micah's grandpa was able to take the whole family horseback riding at a ranch in Arizona. Watching the line of horses walking through the desert, it was remarkable to think back to the days when Micah could not even get out of the car to look at a horse.

Another year the family took an afternoon horseback ride through Glacier National Park. The breathtaking scenery and the large horses made this ride an adventure. Other families in the group of riders were nervous about the trip, and some people decided to back out. Micah rode with confidence, and the whole family thoroughly enjoyed the experience.

DISCUSSION:

When coping with autism, it can be difficult for a family to find fun things they can all do together. Horseback riding was an activity that was exciting, and Micah was leading the way. That other people were not up to the challenge only heightened the family's sense of accomplishment during the trail ride in Glacier Park. All this would not have been possible without therapeutic horseback riding and River Valley Riders.

As a teenager, Micah has also joined a riding program sponsored by Special Olympics for special needs people. This program includes some training in horse care, and it has led to Micah's volunteering to work a few hours at a horse stable near his home.

Therapeutic horseback riding for people with disabilities was developed in the 1960s, although the basic concept was recognized long before that. It is also called hippotherapy or equine assisted therapy.

Therapeutic horseback riding is covered by medical assistance programs in some areas. In other areas, it is considered an alternative therapy and therefore is not covered. If no financial assistance is available, it can be rather expensive.

In her blog titled "Regarding Horses," Jackie Baker writes, "Horses are companion animals. They look to their riders for direction and love. Horses can sense if you are happy, angry, tense, or relaxed, and they respond accordingly. Because of the love and trust they give, they are effective in creating a bond with autistic riders that encourages communication and interaction. They learn to focus on something outside themselves. The movement of the horse is also great for improving circulation, muscle control, and coordination. Most importantly, kids with autism learn to connect with horses, building a trusting relationship that is fun, rewarding, and life changing."

Physically challenged children may not have the potential to ride as well as Micah, but some who have ridden with him had severe physical limitations, yet they enjoyed and benefited from the experience. In some situations, a therapist rides on the horse, holding the child safely in place.

Even if a child never gets on a horse, they benefit from the experience of leading, feeding, petting, and talking to horses. Children thrill as they learn to command and control a huge one thousand pound animal who becomes their friend.

Relationships with animals other than horses should be encouraged. A child with autism can find a friendship with a pet and develop a sense of responsibility while learning to feed and care for it. A movement is underway to train dogs to be companions and guardians of autistic children.

WHAT GRANDPARENTS CAN DO

Micah's experience with horseback riding illustrates the patience required when introducing new things to children with autism. Persistence is often required to break the ice and get them comfortable with a new activity or thing. Time and patience are two things that grandparents may have in more abundance than most people. Parents may have many other responsibilities with jobs, other children, and everyday chores.

Therapeutic horseback riding is an excellent way for grandparents to get involved with horses and their grandchild's social activities. Volunteers of all ages are necessary to keep these programs running. If you know (or can be taught) how to care for horses, there are opportunities to help with transporting, grooming, and tacking. Some brief training is required for leads and side walkers. There are always ways to help out with other tasks that go into making a nonprofit organization function. You can find therapeutic horseback riding in your area through the North American Riding for the Handicapped Association (www.nahra.org) or other organizations.

Providing transportation is something many grandparents can do, whether to a horseback riding camp or other camps often offered for children and teens with autism. Grandparents may help busy parents locate a camp by contacting the local or state autism society.

DEVELOPING NEW INTERESTS

Micah's Favorite Sport—Swimming

"Grab the baby; his head is under water!" Such a shriek was common when Micah's family went to the beach at a small lake near their home. Muriel, at age five, would laugh as she ran and jumped in the shallow water. Micah, at age two, sat listlessly in the sand at the water's edge, timidly splashing his hands in the water. Suddenly, though under the watchful eyes of his parents, he would crawl toward the water, determined to have his head under water. Oddly, Micah seemed to enjoy having his head completely immersed, but had no instinct for lifting his head for needed air.

When it was time to try swimming lessons for Micah, he had not yet been diagnosed with autism, so considerations of special therapies were not a part of his parents' agenda. When they tried a swimming class for tots, Micah did not seem to want to enter the water with other children and their moms. He would not look at the instructor or other children. Here was a child who seemed to enjoy having his head under water, but did not want to be in a pool with other children and adults.

Following the diagnosis of autism at about age three, Micah was started on an early intervention program with the local school system. This did not include swimming, but since his parents now knew activities with groups would not be enjoyable for him, they began thinking of individual sport pursuits. Swimming came to mind since he seemed to enjoy water, albeit on his own terms and not in a group.

Courage Center, where Micah had been enrolled for speech and occupational therapy since age four, has a large warm-water pool with group or individual instructors. Wonderful, colorful plastic toys and floats of all types are available and used to promote swimming with children. At age six, his parents decided to try one-on-one swimming lessons for Micah.

In the beginning of these lessons, Micah would cling to the railing of the steps leading into the pool, arms and legs wrapped firmly around the metal. Instructors would plead, "Micah, come in the water. It's warm, and we have toys to play with." Eventually, gently, they would pry him loose and into the water. Sometimes his mom, sometimes sister Muriel, and at times his grandma would go into the water with him and his instructor, to offer encouragement. Although he was not in a class, others were in the pool, a presence he did not enjoy.

Deborah Townsend remembers her first session with Micah as his new swimming instructor:

> I have fond memories of meeting a cute, blond-haired boy at the edge of the warm, therapeutic, Courage Center pool. Micah was so sweet and shy at the age of six, curious and a little cautious. I grasped immediately that I needed to be gentle and guide him slowly to find his rhythm in the water. My building rapport with him was crucial for developing his trust. One of the amazing qualities of a pool is that it creates a neutral playground. The water is like a great big hug. The warm, humid air surrounding an indoor pool can be calming. I had to minimize my demands and construct a plan customized for Micah. Careful planning and sensitivity to the pace and structure of our sessions provided optimum results.

> So, in reaching that comfortable moment, Micah would let me know it was time to enter the pool. As water exploration advanced to higher levels, I would sometimes invite Muriel into the pool to be playful with her brother. Muriel would demonstrate the freedom water had to offer, and Micah would eventually imitate some basic skills. Goggles became

a fascination; sometimes he wanted to wear them and sometimes not. He would paddle with one hand, holding his nose with the other, so as never to get water up his nostrils. This meant he swam in circles. I wanted Micah to experience the wonder underneath the water, and when the time was right, he became that underwater explorer.

As years passed, he learned to love the pool, swimming under water and even doing laps. Micah was introduced to a snorkel with his mask, but this was discontinued because he wanted his head under water continuously and would not come up to listen to the instructor or practice various swimming strokes. At the end of a lesson, he would cling to the same metal railings, wrapping his arms and legs around them, in an effort to stay in the pool.

As a teenager, Micah enjoys doing as many as fourteen freestyle laps at a time. He loves diving from the surface of the water to pick objects from the bottom of the pool. He eventually graduated to a face mask, freeing his hands from holding his nose. He will stay submerged for such long periods of time that instructors become concerned and may occasionally pull a smiling Micah to the surface. For him, the pressure of the water when submerged is enjoyable, like that big hug Deborah described when he was much younger.

Micah does not enjoy swimming competitions and often shuns cold water pools, especially ones crowded with adults or teeming with children laughing, squealing, and jumping in the water. But he loved swimming at the Courage Center pool, surface diving, staying submerged for long minutes, or trying to tip his instructor or other teenagers off a floating platform. Fear of drowning was no longer an issue.

Micah still swims twice a week at the center and is proficient in freestyle, breaststroke, and backstroke. He has become so strong a swimmer that he can swim the butterfly stroke for two or three pool lengths. Some days he swims with a friend, who is also on the autism spectrum, providing social interaction as well as exercise. He is in rhythm with the water and still loves the big hug it gives him.

DISCUSSION

Children with autism react to water and swimming in many different ways, as do neuro-typical children. Grandparents and parents often report that their children with autism love to swim and play in water, but they must realize special training techniques are required.

A leading cause of accidental deaths among people with autism is drowning. All children must be carefully supervised around pools and water. But children with autism can be particularly vulnerable to accidents because they may wander off and often lack the experience and sensory awareness that triggers an appropriate response to dangerous situations. Micah's early non-reaction to having his head underwater may have been due to a lack of sensory awareness related to autism.

An obvious way to reduce the risk of water-related accidents is swimming lessons. Learning to swim is important for any child, but for children with autism it can be especially meaningful. In addition to the well-known benefits of fun and exercise, swimming lessons provide another opportunity for the child with autism to interact and form a relationship with another person. Swimming is an individual activity, but it has a component of social interaction with others in the water. Later on, competitive swimming can allow the person with autism to compete without the difficulties of interacting with teammates or the opposing team. Therapists suggest the surrounding water satisfies the need for pressure, a feeling of calm and security needed by some people with autism.

Sensory issues at the heart of so much autistic behavior also play a role in swimming. Autistic children may be sensitive to any number of things associated with the water: temperature, the smell of chlorine, water splashing against their skin, noise, having their face and head underwater, and other experiences they might encounter. There are two primary ways to deal with the sensory issues. The first way is to reduce or eliminate the sensation with equipment. Swimming masks, goggles, nose plugs, ear plugs, water shoes, bathing caps, favorite swimsuits may all play a critical role for enabling your grandchild to enter the water. The second way is sensory integration. Children with autism may take a long time and several sessions to become accustomed to the water. A typical progression is to put a hand in the water, then a foot, then sit on the edge of the pool, then splash a little, then slowly get into the pool one stair step at a time. This progression may take several days or months.

Swimming lessons are usually required to make children with autism completely comfortable and safe in the water. Your grandchild may be one who takes to water and learns to swim very easily, but a quick survey of internet blog postings by parents indicates this is not the norm. The swimming lessons need to be adapted to the needs of the child. Standard group lessons often progress too fast and require the students to follow verbal instructions which can be difficult.

Swimming lessons for children with autism should be one-on-one, given by a qualified instructor who has experience teaching special needs children. An experienced teacher will know these children usually require more time to master basic swimming skills. The "sink or swim" approach will result in sinking. Activities must be demonstrated over and over. The teacher should never show what not to do, as children with autism can have difficulty distinguishing the "bad" demonstrations from the "good" demonstrations. Family members may need to occasionally intervene to control unacceptable behavior like drinking the water or abusing pool toys.

Obviously, specialized swimming lessons will be more expensive than conventional swimming lessons. Many school districts and government assistance programs have swimming lessons as part of their special education curriculum and budgets.

All of this sounds like a lot of effort, and it is. But the good news is that most children with autism do show progress, do learn to swim, and do enjoy the water. Swimming can be an activity that is enjoyed individually or with others for a lifetime.

WHAT GRANDPARENTS CAN DO

You must pay special attention to your grandchild with autism around pools and water.

Introduce your grandchild to the water *slowly*. Remember, this will likely take several days or weeks. His parents may not have that kind of time or patience.

Alert friends and other grandchildren that the child with autism needs special monitoring around pools. Expectations in the water cannot be the same as for other children of the same age.

You can buy your grandchild swimming masks, goggles, nose plugs, ear plugs, etc., that will make it easier for him to enter the water. A selection of pool toys can also make learning to swim more fun. Use caution with life jackets, water wings, or other flotation devices that can provide a false sense of security and swimming competence.

Micah, Muriel, and Stuart swimming at the Courage Center pool.

Find out about swimming programs that specialize in teaching children with special needs at your local YMCA, Courage Center, school, etc.

Offer to assist with driving your grandchild to swimming lessons. Again, this will be a long-term commitment that his parents may have trouble keeping by themselves.

Look into programs that can help with the cost of one-on-one swimming lessons.

Have fun with your grandchildren in the water. Your behavior and attention will go a long way toward making them safe and happy in swimming pools and at the beach.

Our experience has involved swimming. Whatever activity becomes important in your grandchild's life, these suggestions can be customized to that activity.

SIBLING RELATIONSHIPS

Micah As a Brother

The school bus driver was waiting for Micah to take a seat before he pulled away from the driveway and made his way to the elementary school Micah and his sister, Muriel, attended. Micah was in third grade, and Muriel was a sixth grader

"Sit down, Micah," the driver yelled, looking into the rear view mirror at bus occupants. "Sit down, or we aren't going anywhere. Sit down, or we'll be late to school."

Micah took a seat near the front of the bus. Muriel was in the rear with her friends. Since he did not make friends well, no one ever shared a seat with Micah, so he sat by himself and for some unknown reason, with his feet in the aisle.

"Micah, get your feet out of the aisle. Someone will trip over them," the bus driver shouted, so loudly everyone on the bus could hear. Micah was not fully verbal at age eight and did not easily understand verbal instructions. The driver yelled at him again, causing stress for Micah. He began to cry and become agitated; melt down began.

This scenario understandably was embarrassing to Muriel, and she felt anger toward the driver. So she moved forward and said, "You aren't handling Micah right. He doesn't understand why you are shouting at him. It would work best if you moved his feet for him. He needs help with some things."

"Don't tell me what to do, young lady. I don't have time to baby kids like that. Now, you sit down, or get off the bus. I'm running late already."

Tearfully, Muriel moved Micah's feet out of the aisle and sat down with him. She didn't want to face her friends right now. The bus drove to the school. Micah's teaching aide met him as usual with a cheery, "Hi Micah!" Then she noted two crying children. "What happened?" she asked. Muriel told the story and said she would like to speak to the principal. Soon the school principal knew the story and after school their mom heard it as well from Muriel. By next day a meeting was called with the bus driver, his supervisor, and Micah's parents.

At the beginning of the school year, bus drivers were made aware of Micah's special needs and that he required individual attention, but this

Micah and Muriel in early elementary grades.

was not always easy with a bus load of energetic children needing to be at school on time. It was determined that providing adult assistance for Micah or sending the bus for handicapped children were the best solutions to the problem. Adult assistance was the least expensive alternative. It was resolved to hire a bus aid to sit with Micah until he was able to understand verbal instructions. Muriel was spared further embarrassment.

DISCUSSION

Sandra L. Harris, Ph.D., begins her book, *Siblings of Children with Autism,* with these comments:

> For more than twenty years I have had the privilege of working with families including a child with autism. They have invited me into their homes, shared their sorrows and triumphs, and trusted me with their children. As I have worked with

these families, and grown older with them, I have had an opportunity to know the siblings as well as parents. In recent years I have felt increasing concern that we do not always meet the needs of siblings in a family with autism.

Micah's parents focused on the needs of his sister, Muriel, as well as they were able. They provided her with voice lessons, rides to school activities, and family vacations centered on her participation in local and national music camps. These are just a few of the ways they focused on her development. They dealt with her stresses as sister to a challenged brother as well as they were able. However, my conversations with her have revealed some thoughts and concerns, especially about her future as Micah's sister.

When Muriel was eighteen and about to enter a small liberal arts college in Pennsylvania, I asked if I might interview her with questions concerning her life with Micah. She was very receptive. "Is there anything about Micah's behavior that annoys you," I asked, realizing all siblings irk one another to some degree.

"Yes," she replied," I don't like it when he paces, runs in circles, squeals, and shakes his hands. Also, when he repeats and repeats lines he has heard on TV, especially commercials, of which he really doesn't understand the meaning. There are some common awareness issues he doesn't seem to understand, like standing on my feet or slamming a door in my face when I am behind him. He will chant 'All right, all right. I get it, I get it,' when he is corrected or asked to do something. I think he is smarter than we realize. He 'gets' some things, but uses his autism to get his way or avoid obeying."

Muriel thinks sometimes she gets in trouble for something Micah has done, perhaps a common sibling complaint. "Mom takes his side, and he is disciplined differently than I am. If I try to correct him on something, my parents say, 'That's not your job.' I think he can use his autism to be manipulative. It's like if we have inter-sibling issues, I can't chew him out; I can't express my thoughts to him."

"Do you think in any way, you have been a positive influence in Micah's life?" I asked.

"Well, yes. I give him an interaction besides my parents. We are so distant, though, it is hard to say how great an influence I have been. He doesn't pay attention to me; he seems unaware of my presence most of the time."

"Has it helped you in any way to have a special needs brother?"

"It has, because exposure to special needs persons doesn't shock me. Whether it is someone with a mental or physical need, I'm very tolerant of them. I'm also impatient with others who are intolerant of people with disabilities."

When Micah was to enter junior high school the fall after Muriel left the school, she asked her friends in the class behind her to report if they ever observed someone being mean to Micah. This was because she witnessed some inconsideration on the part of students to other special needs kids.

"Have other kids treated you differently because of Micah?"

"They may think of me differently, like, 'You've been through some stuff,' but never, 'Oh, you poor thing.'"

"How do you think you and Micah will relate as adults?"

"It worries me, especially if I am in charge of him as an adult. He doesn't listen to me. He doesn't give a hoot about me. He needs to have some connection to me. Eventually, I will have to take care of Micah in some way. I think that is my responsibility. Maybe he will become more self-sufficient, but it doesn't appear so now. I won't be a sister that shoves him off someplace, but I don't really want him in my home all the time when my parents can no longer care for him. He receives lots of good therapy, swimming lessons, and all that at Courage Center, but I don't want to sit there waiting for him the rest of my life. However, I do want to help make decisions about his future. I will want him to be in a good safe place where he can be happy."

WHAT GRANDPARENTS CAN DO

Grandparents can observe and listen. Sometimes grandparents see frustration on the part of siblings in a family with a brother or sister on the autism spectrum. By listening, a grandparent gives siblings a way to vent their disappointments in dealing with their situation. It is not advisable to discipline grandchildren unless that action is supported by their parents. Just being a sounding board can be helpful.

Scheduling overnight stays and outings with a brother or sister can be very helpful to the child with autism and the parents. Siblings of children with autism need time away with understanding and loving people, just as parents can benefit from a reprieve now and then.

Grandparents can become well informed about autism. This enables them to more intelligently deal with complaints they may hear from a brother or sister. Such complaints should not be encouraged but dealt with as skillfully as possible when they do occur. It is important to remember that siblings love their brother or sister, but don't have the maturity or skills to understand how to handle their frustrations unless they are adults.

Everyone in a family affected by autism could use a support system, including our family. We found it helpful to meet periodically with another family similar to ours including a grandchild with autism. You may contact a local or state autism society and inquire if support groups are available for siblings, or you could help form one.

RELATIONSHIPS IN THE EXTENDED FAMILY

We Visit Micah's Cousins in Kansas City

"One-hundred-ninety-eight miles to go! One-hundred-ninety-four miles to go!" It was sounding like a chant. Micah announced the miles remaining to Kansas City frequently and loudly. His excitement was intensifying as the distance decreased. It was approximately four hundred miles from St. Paul, Minnesota, to our Kansas City destination, and he updated us every five miles—or less. A Global Positioning System, commonly known as a GPS, was apparently new to Micah. His grandfather taught him how to program the system before we began our trip. Now, his long, lanky fourteen-year-old body was wedged into the passenger seat, knees against the dashboard and spikes of blond hair brushing the sun roof. While his grandfather drove, Micah was mesmerized by the GPS. Now and then he would look out the window and comment on some passing scenery; then his eyes returned to the computerized instrument.

Growing weary of the frequent mileage proclamations, I called from the back seat, "Micah, would you like to play on your Game Boy?" Usually amusing himself with the Game Boy was discouraged, because it could consume hours of his time and he became oblivious to everything else around him. However, a respite from the GPS would be good for all of us, I reasoned.

"No thank you, I want to watch the GPS," was the polite reply.

"Well, alright, but let me know if you change your mind," I responded, hopefully.

Late in the afternoon, we arrived at our destination, the home of our daughter and family. Micah bolted out of the car, running and hopping to the front door. His cousin Hannah responded to the doorbell, followed by her brothers Connor and Taylor. Our son-in-law, Jon, and daughter, Natalyn, also crowded around the doorway. Jasmine, the family's black lab, jumped and scooted about the hallway. It was a joyous reunion. Warm hugs were shared by everyone, but I noticed Micah stepping back toward the door, earlier excitement fading from his face. "Say hello to everyone," I whispered to him.

Micah stiffly shook hands with each person and chanted, in a slightly monotone voice, "It's good to see you; it's been a long time." The same exact words were repeated to each person as he looked off to the side of them rather than into their faces.

"Hey, Micah, how was the trip?"

"Good." Then, although Jasmine was jumping, wanting to play, and everyone was eager to talk, Micah was overcome with shyness. He dashed downstairs to the lower level of the house where he knew there would be a television set and solitude. It was heart wrenching to know how he had looked forward to seeing his cousins, but now could not deal with the occasion. Later, his cousin Connor went downstairs to be with Micah. There may have been little conversation, but there was togetherness, which was good. Fortified by the calmness and quietness of the lower room and Connor's caring presence, Micah was later able to rejoin the family, eat dinner with everyone, and converse a bit.

A family bowling event the next day was enjoyable for Micah. Some unusual interest in competing with his Uncle Jon, a professional athlete, was refreshing to witness. His inhibitions were at low ebb in the bowling alley. He relaxed and was able to enjoy his cousins, even though from time to time he paced around behind the seating area or became distracted by screens flashing animated responses to strikes and spares.

Some hikes around the neighborhood that weekend and sight-seeing in and around Kansas City were highlights for Micah. He enjoyed eating in restaurants with the family, provided they offered French fries, plain spaghetti, or cheese pizza. A memorable time for his Aunt Natalyn occurred early one morning when, alone with him at breakfast, she was able to have a conversation with Micah. They chatted about his school, subjects he liked, and horse riding activities

After "Good-bye," "When will we see you again?" "Thanks for coming," we started back to the Minneapolis area. For a while Micah was content with his Game Boy. However, after a few miles, he asked, "Grandpa, can I set the GPS?"

"Sure, you can."

Shortly after, Micah informed us, "Three hundred forty-nine miles to Minneapolis!"

DISCUSSION

In this story, Micah exhibits some of the same characteristics as when he was a little boy at the Christmas party. The inability to cope with a number of individuals at his cousins' doorway was one. He, of course, did not show the terror he displayed at encountering a wall of strangers, but he was unable to cope, momentarily, with meeting a group of people, even though he knew them well.

Greeting each person in the family with the same phrase was perhaps the result of coaching by a therapist at a class offered to special education students on etiquette. Such a salutation may seem very stilted, but served as a good "crutch," enabling Micah to come forward, shake hands, and lose some inhibitions.

He sought isolation. An off-limits playroom served that purpose at the Christmas party, now the sanctuary he needed was a downstairs recreation room. As a teenager there was no picture map to guide him through this social situation as there had been for the rooms and activities at the pre-school event as a three year old.

At age fourteen, competition was still not something Micah enjoyed. Certainly he had no interest in team sports of any kind. Despite his height, basketball did not intrigue him, nor soccer, hockey, or football. Even board games or card games with another person or group did not capture his interest. When skiing, he would not wish to compete in races or slalom events. He also enjoyed golf but did not keep score. Only in bowling was "beating" another person enjoyable.

WHAT GRANDPARENTS CAN DO

If you and your grandchild enjoy traveling together, it can be rewarding. Preparation is important so everyone can enjoy this time together. It is best to let the child wear whatever clothing is comfortable. Many autistic children are sensitive to certain fiber textures and have strong preferences for what they want to wear. Especially with small children, take favorite toys, blankets, or pillows.

Grandparents perform a most valuable function when they assume the role of family bridge. Rarely-seen relatives will desperately want to communicate with the autistic child, but may not know what to talk about or how to approach him. Concentrating on bridging this gap can make family gatherings meaningful and pleasant for all. Bridging can be done by introducing conversation and activities in which the child is capable of participating and willing to join. Family conversation in advance of get-togethers, sharing magazine clippings about autism, suggesting pertinent websites and books such as this one, ease entry into the child's world

Autism Spectrum Quarterly is a magazine filled with helpful articles geared toward parents and extended family members as well as teachers and therapists. Subscribing and sharing with family is something grandparents could do. Visit the magazine website at www.ASQuarterly.com.

COMMUNITY RELATIONSHIPS

Micah's Family Builds a Team

It is a cool, sunny morning in April. An SUV wends its way slowly down the long graveled lane to Micah's home in the country, avoiding potholes created by spring rains. Micah is waiting, pacing up and down, singing in a high-pitched voice, sometimes skipping on the sidewalk leading from the front door to the driveway. Saturday morning at ten o'clock is a high point of the week for him, because that is when he goes bowling with his friend Neil.

Neil is the retired customer service manager of a large corporation in St. Paul. He met Micah at River Valley Riders, as a volunteer assisting special needs youth learning to ride horseback. As he walked beside the horse Micah was riding around an outdoor ring five years ago, Neil asked "What do you like to do, Micah, besides horseback riding? Do you like to play basketball or soccer?"

"No," came a quick retort. "I like to go bowling."

"So do I, Micah. Would you like to go with me sometime?"

"Yes."

Neil spoke with Micah's parents. A Saturday morning ritual began, as did a friendship lasting over the years.

When Neil and Micah arrive at the bowling alley, Micah likes to order French fries or pizza. This he has done so regularly, the bowling attendant asks him when he enters, "What will it be today, Micah, pizza or French fries?" Neil waits patiently as Micah takes time out to eat his treat, even if the bowling has begun.

Neil does not give Micah instructions on how to bowl, but gives simple, subtle hints. When their bowling relationship began, Micah walked up to the edge of the alley, ball in hand, and dropped it. "Plunk." The ball slowly meandered down the alley, swerving from bumper to bumper. Bumpers are rails raised on either side of the alley to assist beginning bowlers. Spectators held their breath and silently urged the ball down toward the pins. To cheer and encourage the ball out loud would have embarrassed and intimidated Micah. If any pins went down, he was happy and excited, and jumped up and down. He especially enjoyed watching the pin count and the movements of the cartoon characters on the overhead TV screen. In the early days of his bowling experience, the total score seemed meaningless to him

Micah's bowling skills have improved in five years' time. The bumpers are no longer needed. He still walks to the start of the alley and swings the ball several times before releasing it toward the pins. Now, he will shout, "I got a spare," or "I got a strike," when that happens; he skips his tall body up and down in the small area behind the alley. Over the years it has become more agreeable to him for spectators to celebrate his good fortunes if he has a strike or spare. His scoring is erratic, but the total score is meaningful, and he likes to win. One time he met his ultimate goal, to beat Neil. Who was most excited when that happened, Micah or Neil? It was hard to tell.

Noise levels in bowling alleys are high, with balls slamming into pins, knocking them about like toothpicks, and jovial laughter from the bar area reaching to the alleys. Children are laughing and shouting, parents are urging their children to turn their wrists, and teenagers in adjacent alleys are boisterous with their peers. Usually loud noise hurts Micah's ears; he covers them with his hands and shies away from noisy environments. But the love of bowling calms him and supersedes his discomfort.

Bright neon lights flashing in bowling alleys surround Micah with distraction. His attention is absorbed by light on the TV and movie screens, computer screens above the alleys, and flashing advertisements when he is not up to bowl.

"Micah, Micah, it's your turn! Come on, let's go!" is a common refrain when his family bowls with him during the week. Such urgings cause him to turn toward the ball carrier, but he may still have eyes glued to some lighted, moving distraction. Seldom does he watch the play of his co-players.

At age sixteen, Micah does not yet fully appreciate his friend Neil, at least he is not able to verbalize his gratitude. This inability makes Neil's weekly contribution of time with Micah even more amazing and treasured by his family. Neil is one of a great team of volunteers who have given their time over the years to nurture Micah and give his family reprieve from the intensity of parenting a child with autism.

DISCUSSION

Extended family, friends, and neighbors can do much to help parents cope with the challenges of raising a child with autism. Informing and educating such a community is a challenge, especially if denial or misinformation is a part of the picture.

Micah participates in a Special Olympics skiing program.

As a grandparent, I have observed the construction of a successful volunteer team. Some participate at the initiative of Micah's parents. Friends at their church and school also contribute. A five-member panel assembled and presented ideas for building such a team at a Minnesota Autism Conference in April 2009. Two members were parents of children with autism, two had worked professionally with families, and one was a committed volunteer to special needs children. All have reached out to families affected by autism, and each panel member had touched Micah's life in some way. This panel was asked to discuss ways to recruit and educate family and friends about autism so they may become comfortable being team members.

Assistance is available for families within most communities. It varies from area to area, and an overburdened parent may not have time or skills to work through the daunting process of obtaining aid. Someone outside the family can be helpful in obtaining assistance from agencies, churches, and organizations. Recruiting team members who are both willing and capable of working directly with a child is a relief to parents. However, children with behavioral problems can be intimidating to those willing to help. Training assistants is an important part of team building. Direct involvement with the child with autism is not the only way to help. When friends and relatives recognize the restrictions autistic children place on a family, they may recognize that helping with household chores or giving attention to siblings in the home is needed.

Panel members suggested contacting staff members at a family's place of worship and involving the child with autism in community programs designed to help special needs children. Micah's parents have enrolled him in several Special Olympics programs offering horseback riding, golf, bowling, and skiing. Micah has received swimming therapy and instruction for many years at Courage Center, where he also has benefited from speech and occupational therapy.

Most children with autism require babysitters with special qualifications. Unless a teenage babysitter is trained and is unusually mature, parents would not feel comfortable calling the high school student down the street. Some understanding of autism and a great deal of patience are required for babysitters. Recommendations for care givers can come from a church, the family's social worker, friends, or extended family.

As the child with autism reaches pre-teen and teen ages, the problem becomes more challenging. Many parents are comfortable leaving their typical thirteen-, fourteen-, or fifteen-year-old children unattended. That is probably unacceptable for an autistic child with limited communication skills. If the person with autism is considered vulnerable, parents will need to provide supervision at all times up through age eighteen and very possibly beyond.

Teenage babysitters are probably not a good choice to watch another teenager close to their own age, especially one with autism. A trained adult may be the only choice. Such an adult may be very difficult to find, unless it is a family member or exceptionally good friend. A solution may be for parents of autistic persons to exchange babysitting or teen watching.

An interesting phenomenon associated in working with autism is the effect it has on volunteers. The world of autism has an aura of mysticism. It can be captivating, rewarding, and stimulating to team participants.

WHAT GRANDPARENTS CAN DO

While our discussion has focused on developing a team of people outside the immediate family, grandparents obviously can be an important part of that team as well. You already know your strengths and abilities, and you probably can think of ways to share them with your grandchild. The fact you have read this far into the book indicates you are willing to help. You have the opportunity to fill a unique and important place in the life of your grandchild.

It is often not enough to simply volunteer to babysit or help with your autistic grandchild. While this may be helpful and appreciated by the parents, it will not lead to the type of regular interaction and bonding experience illustrated in the story. A simple offer of assistance still requires the parents to schedule in advance, make a phone call or multiple calls to reach you, and hope that your schedule coincides with theirs. This leads to missed opportunities for you, your grandchild, and the parents. A better approach is to set a regular time when everyone is usually available, and then to have everyone keep that appointment as much as possible. It gives everyone something to look forward to, and it relieves the burden and awkwardness of having to approach someone to ask for time in their busy schedule. The appointment does not have to go on forever. It is probably better to put an end date on things (i.e. just until school starts again, or until December when things usually get busy at work) so that everyone can move on to something different.

It is a fact of life that some grandparents may not have the time or energy to offer direct involvement with their autistic grandchild. Babysitting children on the autism spectrum can be physically demanding, depending on the child's level of disability. A grandparent may have limited physical abilities of their own. Often situations arise that require unusual patience and understanding of the child's taste for certain foods or lack of need for sleep.

Even if you cannot be directly involved with your grandchild, you can still be part of his family's team building efforts. Your children may not have time to seek out even one assistant, let alone a team of volunteers. You could offer a service by phoning local city and county resources. A contact with the state autism society may prove helpful in seeking assistance for your child's family. Financial aid, if needed, can be found at the county or state government levels in most states.

It requires a team to raise a child on the autism spectrum. Grandparents can be on the team at whatever level they are able to participate.

TRAVEL EXPERIENCES

We Go to Washington, D.C.

When our grandchildren reach pre-teen age, we take them on a grandparent trip. We took the oldest of our five to the East Coast eight years ago. Three years later, two twelve-year-old cousins took the same trip. Our last two grandchildren, Micah and his cousin, Hannah, reached ages thirteen and twelve in 2009. We did not know if it was fair to expect Hannah to share a trip with Micah, since he has limited abilities. We decided to allow Hannah to solve the dilemma.

While visiting our daughter's family in Kansas City we queried Hannah. "Would you like to share a trip to Washington, D.C., with Micah or go with us on one of your own next year?"

After a long pause and a sigh she responded, "I can't decide. Can I tell you tomorrow?"

Next day, we met with Hannah in the living room to receive her positive reply. We were delighted. Since she never has lived near Micah, and spends only a few days with him each summer, she has had limited experience with him. "Micah can be challenging at times. It will require patience to travel with him, but it will also be fun if we plan carefully," we explained to Hannah.

"I know," she replied. "I want to write down a few things about autism." She left the room, returning with a page from a notebook divided into two columns. In one column she wanted to list characteristics of persons with autism, in the other column characteristics of people with no autism. "I know Micah doesn't talk much, and he's picky about food. Sometimes he walks back and forth in a room and shakes his hands. I have heard him talking to himself in a squeaky voice. Now, what else should I expect?" We felt immense pride toward Hannah when she asked us to help her understand Micah. It was important that she feel comfortable with Micah's mannerisms during the trip

"You have been very observant, Hannah. There are some responsibilities we must all think about during this trip. Someone will have to stay near him when we are crossing streets because he sometimes forgets to watch for traffic. In museums and large buildings in D.C. he may get distracted and wander away, so someone must be at his side at all times, especially in crowded places. Micah can learn a great deal from you, Hannah, if you are patient and talk to him without expecting him to reply the same way other kids would."

The departure day in June arrived. We were all in high spirits. Micah had flown previously with his family, so we knew the flight would go well. Micah's parents tell of the time the family was on a plane going through some bad weather. The other passengers on the flight looked concerned as the plane jolted and lurched during the descent to the runway. Micah, age five, was giggling and laughing, thoroughly enjoying the ride. "That makes my butt dizzy," he exclaimed loudly during one bumpy episode. After a safe landing, everyone looked back at Micah as they moved forward to get off the plane. They smiled at the little boy who brought some humor and a new perspective to a tense situation.

Now older, his delight when the plane took off and when it landed was that expected of a much younger child. As the engines accelerated and the plane shuttered for take off, Micah squealed, "We're going into the air now!" Intense noise, such as the roar of the engines, usually hurts his ears, but the thrill of flying apparently distracted him from the discomfort. As we approached the landing strip in Washington, D.C., he again gleefully cried out, "There's the Washington Monument! I see the Washington Monument!"

Reservations at a Holiday Inn in a section of Washington now inhabited by young professionals proved to be a good choice. A breakfast buffet each morning was more elaborate than expected at a motel. Micah shunned most offerings at the buffet, loading his plate with only French toast the first morning. The second day his choice was a heap of bacon. The third, a large pile of pancakes. "Micah, why don't you have some bacon with your pancakes," Hannah asked.

"Because, I had my bacon yesterday," he replied.

Surrounding the motel were wonderful neighborhood restaurants with interesting menus. We encouraged Hannah to try items she would not ordinarily eat, which she enjoyed. As expected, Micah would not be adventuresome. His lunches were commonly huge plates of French fries, nothing else. For dinners he would have his favorite, cheese pizza, or spaghetti without sauce and only Parmesan cheese. His beverage of choice was always water, no ice. We knew Micah's mom and dad usually cajoled him into eating something more, such as a few peas or green grapes to supplement a high carbohydrate diet, but we were all on vacation and ate what pleased us.

Hannah, Micah, and Grandma Syl at the Smithsonian Museum.

Four days ended quickly. Micah did not mind large crowds, only shying away if a stranger spoke to him. He liked reading street signs and following maps. We visited the Museum of Natural History where recorded sounds of crickets annoyed Micah. Hannah loved gift shops everywhere, especially at the Holocaust Museum where she selected a copy of *The Diary of Anne Frank*. Micah showed little interest in gift shops. We bought each child a disposable camera. Hannah carefully planned taking her photos, while Micah snapped all his from inside a taxi cab, in a ten-minute time period.

"Micah, you used up all your pictures," Hannah exclaimed, "Now you won't have any for later."

"I know. I wanted to take my pictures now."

Travel Experiences | 111

A day touring the Capitol building with its ornate statues and massive paintings intrigued all of us. The crowds of visitors were huge, and we feared Micah would feel overwhelmed. He cringed only when we passed security points, and guards asked questions of each of us. One-on-one encounters with strangers caused him to look to the floor, unable to answer their questions. He showed no interest in the House of Representatives when we were privileged to briefly sit in its chambers and hear then Speaker of the House Nancy Pelosi addressing the assembled lawmakers. A year later, Hannah recalled being in the House of Representatives as a highlight of the trip. Micah recalled, "We were in the Capitol building, and it was big."

Micah can easily become engrossed in a Game Boy. This is good when times are boring, but not when we need his attention. One morning he was especially glued to his Game Boy and would not surrender it as we crossed a busy street with many lanes of traffic. In desperation for his safety, I grabbed the game piece from his hands. He responded with a meltdown, displaying anger toward me. For the remainder of the day he would not speak to me or look in my direction, insisting on walking a distance of some feet away. In retrospect, I realize Micah should have been prepared for a day without his toy, with explanation as to why we would leave it in the hotel. A meltdown may have been prevented. By the next morning he either forgot the episode or forgave me.

"What was your favorite of all the things we saw or did?" we asked during dinner the final day. "Was it visiting the Washington Monument? Visiting the Smithsonian Museums?" Micah had talked of little else than the Washington Monument during the plane ride, and since he squealed with glee when he spotted it during our descent into D.C., we assumed that would be his favorite. "Did you like seeing the Lincoln Memorial, or walking past the White House?"

Micah chimed in with Hannah, "No. It was riding the Metro!"

We had observed Micah's delight when our subway ticket was swallowed in a slot near the turnstile and suddenly spit out the other side. He had squealed when the train seemed to slam into a darkened tunnel only to emerge rapidly in lights at the next station. "Oh no, is it over already?" quizzed a disappointed Hannah when we had to quickly disembark.

These two grandchildren, so different in character, had after all agreed on their favorite adventure in D.C.—riding the Metro.

DISCUSSION

It is fortunate for our family Micah loves to travel. Perhaps it is because he has been exposed to travel his whole life, or it may be due to his special interest in geography. He enjoys looking at maps and at a young age not only wanted a map of New York City but also asked to go there. Children with autism can develop a special interest, even a fixation, on a place, event, or collection of items.

Micah also has a keen sense of spatial concepts and shows an unusual sense of direction. This would not be true of all children with autism, but often they do display an unusual ability or intense interest in a subject.

Becoming separated is a great concern for anyone responsible for a child away from home. For children with autism, the risk is magnified because some have a propensity for leaving the watchful eye of adults, either willingly or unwittingly. When children with autism do get lost, they are at increased risk because they may have difficulty approaching strangers, even police officers. The child may not be able to communicate that they are lost, where they are going, or from where they have come.

Children with autism can be subject to sensory overload. That may have been a problem for Micah in the Capitol building. The combination of large crowds and an overwhelming amount of statuary and pictures kept him from enjoying any one thing as we rushed along on the tour. If he was overloaded, he handled it well and did not display frustration by way of a meltdown or a display of physical signs of disconnection. If that had occurred, his grandfather or I would have removed him to a quiet place until he was able to deal with his stress.

WHAT GRANDPARENTS CAN DO

Traveling with an autistic grandchild may be an unrealistic venture in some families. Try an overnight trip somewhere before attempting a vacation of several days—sort of a trial run.

If you do plan an extended time with a grandchild with autism, prepare yourself for frustrations that could arise with any child, such as homesickness. With a special needs grandchild, make sure his parents brief you—including instructions on administrating medications they send along. A letter authorizing medical attention signed by the parents is a good idea as well. To enter certain sections of the U.S. Capitol, we needed a copy of the children's birth certificates.

If meltdowns are a particular problem for a grandparent relating to a grandchild with autism, you may wish to talk to their parents who have surely had to deal with the same problem. Another avenue is to ask the child's parents if you can speak to a therapist who works with your grandchild and others on the spectrum for ideas when such situations arise. There are many books with sections on the subject of meltdowns. One which we found helpful is *Adolescents on the Spectrum* by Chantal Sicile-Kira. She is also the author of *Autism Spectrum Disorders*.

My husband and I have learned that meltdowns, such as the one experienced with Micah on the street in Washington, D.C., can be prevented by carefully preparing the child ahead of time. This can include outlining in detail what is planned for a day's activities, or taking only toys or objects that will not have to be taken from the child during the day.

Diet can be a problem when traveling with an autistic grandchild. It is best to check with their parents before beginning an outing or trip. Carrying appropriate food with you may be the solution for day trips; you should not try to introduce new foods when away from his home environment.

Clearly you must gauge the risk of your grandchild wandering off or running away from you. In any case, some advanced preparation and training will help you and your grandchild find each other again. Some ideas and strategies we have used include:

- Hold your grandchild's hand in crowded situations and when crossing streets. It will become natural after a while. As long as you are not tugging at each other, no one will notice or make you feel awkward, even if the child is older. Stay near them at all times.

- Point out people who can help if you get separated. Make sure your grandchild can identify police officers and security guards.

- Instruct your grandchild that they must tell someone immediately if they get lost. It is not OK to wait or to go look for Grandpa or Grandma. Some children with autism have been known to hide from authority figures trying to find them.

- Write your name and phone number on a piece of paper or business card, and put it in the child's pocket. Instruct them to show it to a helpful adult if you get separated.

- Dress your grandchild in distinctive clothing. They will be easier for you and others to spot. Also, it is surprising how quickly you can forget what they were wearing if it is not distinctive.

- Give your grandchild a cell phone. It can be inexpensive with few features and a limited calling plan. Program your phone number into the address list, or if you are like most grandparents, have your grandchild do the programming. Teach your grandchild how to dial your cell phone number and/or 911.

- All cell phones have global positioning system capacity so that the phone can be located. Ask your telephone company what is required to turn it on.

- Always rehearse what to say to a police officer, helpful adult, or 911 operator.

Our trip to Washington went surprisingly well. Much of the success is credited to our granddaughter, Hannah, who displayed a very mature attitude when coping with her cousin's special needs and challenges.

RELIGIOUS TRADITION AND TRAINING

Micah Is Confirmed

During a warm afternoon in October, Micah's grandfather and I perspired in a warm, crowded church. His parents, Susan and Stuart, and Susan's parents, the Baxters, shared our bench. Micah's sister, Muriel, and several aunts, uncles, and cousins were seated on pews behind us. "Do you think he will do it? It's hard to imagine he will," were the whispers back and forth as we awaited the procession of confirmands to begin. This day was the culmination of two and one-half years of catechism study, as it is called in Lutheran churches, the preparation for confirmation. Students would now become adult members of the congregation.

"I can't believe he even completed the study," I marveled.

"He is changing," offered Micah's grandfather.

"But he is still so shy and withdrawn among strangers. How can he deal with this huge crowd and the loud organ music? And he will dislike wearing a gown!"

"Well, he likes this church. The adults and his peers have treated him kindly. It's sure to help," Grandpa suggested.

I reminisced on the day I learned Micah's parents were intending to send him to classes preparing him for confirmation in this large congregation. Through study, I had learned that abstract concepts could be difficult for the autistic mind to grasp. This might include difficulties understanding faith, heaven, Christ's presence at the sacrament of communion, and the Triune God. Bible stories about Jesus' life on earth could be comprehensible for him.

Classes of seventy-five or more did not seem like a situation Micah would agree to be part of or enjoy. Then I learned the church staff divided the large group into small circles for study, service, and recreation. They had engaged a woman, Mary Williams, who understood autism and had agreed to take Micah into her small group of five boys. The seventh graders were chosen because they already knew Micah or agreed to befriend him. They learned he loved to bowl, so it was decided that would be their recreational choice.

This effort was immensely successful. That spring Micah participated in an art project with his small group. For his project he chose to paint Christian symbols on white canvas. Among the representations were a cross, a chalice, and a Bible. A time was selected for all students to speak briefly about their project to the large group. To everyone's amazement, Micah stood, did not face the class, but in a very soft voice, explained his art work to the entire group of nearly 100 kids. We were not present that day, but we heard reports of tears choking parents and group leaders.

The heat in the church persisted as folks fanned themselves with handout flyers listing names of all the confirmands. "Is the air conditioning working?" we murmured. At the appointed time, the organ music changed to a processional piece, we all stood, and the students slowly entered the sanctuary. Eager parents and relatives craned their necks to catch sight of their beloved teenager. "Where is Micah? Oh, no. He's not going to participate!" I worried to his grandfather.

"Just wait. More are coming," an equally nervous grandfather retorted.

And then, there he was. A classmate was carefully guiding him along the aisle. He was there, in his white robe, moving down the aisle among a group of classmates. Shivers of joy and pride surged through me, and a faint gasp emitted from Micah's parents and relatives.

The service was long—very long in my opinion. As we continued to fan ourselves, I thought of the discomfort the teenagers must feel, in their robes, seated in a semi-circle behind the altar. I searched for Micah among the throng of white. He was sitting quietly; a classmate next to him seemed to be whispering to him frequently, perhaps informing him of events happening or to come in the service. For one hour we listened to selected students give testimonials to their faith. The remaining hour was devoted to small groups coming to the front of the altar, facing hundreds of people. Each youth received a blessing as parents and relatives came forward to surround their special teenager.

Micah's group was to be last. "Well, he will never do that," I whispered to Grandpa.

"Just wait. Be patient."

When his group was called to come forward, Micah was guided along. We left our seats to surround him in front of the altar, and lay our hands on his shoulders and arms. Tears were difficult to control. Micah did not look at any of us, but hurried back to his seat when his blessing was completed.

Was it a blessing or a miracle occurring that day?

DISCUSSION

Sunday worship and participation in classes has been a valued channel to a faith in Christ and belief in God for Micah's family. He was born into a family with a strong religious tradition. He had two grandparents, one on each side of the family, who had training and professional experience working in Protestant congregations. His maternal grandfather, Harlan Baxter, is a Methodist pastor, and I, his paternal grandmother, served as a parish worker in Lutheran churches for many years.

Micah's mom and dad enjoyed attending church together since they first met in college. Naturally they wanted to continue, introducing their children to the joys found in a life of faith, Christian community, and an understanding of religious tradition and worship. Micah's autism created a serious challenge to family worship attendance.

When Micah was an infant and toddler, he would spend time in the church nursery, along with other young children. The nursery staff soon learned how to accommodate a child who would play with only one or two toys. They learned not to worry if he repeatedly shook or rotated the toys back and forth, over and over.

Occasionally Micah's parents would try to take him to a church service. Early on there were crying episodes. He had to be taken out of the sanctuary to the "crying bench," where parents could watch the service through a window without disturbing the rest of the worshipers. When he reached age two, he actively resisted going into the sanctuary by bracing his little arms and legs against the doors in a panicked attempt to stay outside. His parents tried all sorts of distractions like books, crayons, and toys. Eventually the family resigned themselves to the crying bench even before the service started.

Shortly after that, Micah was diagnosed with autism, and it became apparent why he resisted going to a church service. Services had everything irritating to his young autistic senses: crowds, amplified voices, singing, people wearing robes (he developed a fear of anyone wearing a costume or unusual clothing), intense music, and a requirement to sit still. To him, the sanctuary was a torture chamber, and naturally he did everything he could to resist entering.

Micah's attention span was very short, so as he grew older, sitting in a Sunday school class was not beneficial for him and caused disruption for other children. He was not ready to be in a classroom with other children his age. He could not follow instructions, did not like to listen to stories, and singing songs was very unpleasant for him. Most volunteer teachers are not equipped to deal with special needs children in a one-hour Sunday morning session. When he was in elementary grades, there were attempts on the part of their church to provide volunteer mentors to be with Micah on some Sunday mornings. When a session was designed around an activity rather than sitting still and discussing a Bible story, chances of holding his attention improved. Most Sundays Micah's parents felt the effort was not worth the small amount he might benefit from Sunday school classes. They were losing an important part of family life to autism.

Dealing with an autistic child in a public or semi-private place is a huge challenge for parents. Did members of Micah's congregation think his behavior was due to bad parenting? The sideways looks and grimaces are difficult for young moms and dads, trying to do a good job of parenting.

There were reports of congregations in our metro area that had asked parents with autistic children not to attend services because of the disruption caused by the youngsters. Micah's mother once attended a large church in another city. Knowing that Micah could not be left in the nursery, she took him to the service. When he began to act up, the minister stopped his sermon, singled them out, and asked Susan to please remove Micah to the nursery. She was deeply embarrassed. Several members of the congregation later apologized to her for the minister's behavior.

When Micah was ten, the family decided to find a new church home. They had a few basic criteria for selecting a new church, such as denomination and location. Over a series of Sundays, they visited various worship services. Each time, Micah had great difficulty entering the church and sitting through a service. One Sunday, they attended Trinity Lutheran Church in Stillwater, Minnesota. To their disbelief and gratitude, Micah walked into the sanctuary and sat quietly through the service reading a book. Later, Muriel found friends from her school who attended Trinity. The family had found a new church home!

Trinity Lutheran's summer drive-in worship service, outside of Stillwater, at an abandoned drive-in theater site, is especially comfortable for Micah and his family. The bulletin hand-out states, "We gladly welcome dog members of your family at the drive-in worship, however please keep your dog on a six-foot leash at all times." How could a service be more welcoming and casual?

Picture this: On a fine summer Sunday morning, Micah paces back and forth beside the family car as hymns are sung, sermon and prayers delivered over a loud speaker. He is smiling, but apparently listening because he joins his family in the car now and then and asks questions about something in the sermon. Some babies and toddlers are in their pajamas, busily munching on Cheerios and sipping milk from bottles or training cups, sitting in their car seats or on the grass beside the family car. Older children wander to a swing set so as to be more comfortable during the sermon. Coffee, juice, and homemade scones are available before the service begins.

There is an antique car or two, some motorcycles, and at times a horse tethered to a post among the nearly 200 vehicles. Some folks sit in lawn chairs, others on blankets, singing and listening. Those staying in their cars can listen in on radios tuned to a special frequency. The worship leaders are standing on a platform beneath the ragged, unused movie screen rising many feet behind them.

Following the sermon, Micah joins the long line of worshipers moving forward to partake in the Lord's Supper. He does not eat the bread or drink the wine, but receives a blessing. His mom and dad think that is O.K. In his own way he participates.

The summer worship services are ideal for Micah and his family. Following the service pancakes may be served, or on Sundae Sundays, ice cream with a choice of toppings. Each summer one Sunday is set aside for blessing animals. Pets of every kind are welcome to receive a blessing. Micah could bring one or two of the chickens he is tending. Or he may bring a duck Muriel is keeping for a science project. Micah can comprehend this type of activity. He seems happy at this service. He can move about, the music is not too loud, and since people are spread out in and around their cars, he does not have to deal with crowds crushing in on him. For both Micah and his family, it is a peaceful worship experience.

Some children and teenagers on the autism spectrum could not function in religious instruction as well as Micah. This would be understandable, and other arrangements may be made with the help of a church or synagogue. Sometimes only one-on-one instruction may serve the child. Of course, this is a highly personal matter, and my story is offered only as that—a personal account of what worked for Micah. Bible stories and spiritual concepts can be presented in a variety of ways, such as videos, which may be available through a church or synod headquarters. At Micah's church they put out a request for volunteers to work with a special needs student. Several special education teachers from the congregation were delighted to have the opportunity to use their educational training in a religious setting. Some religious publishers are a good resource for materials to use with special needs children.

Churches, particularly small congregations, may struggle with providing resources to educate and engage just one or two special needs children. By calling on the resources of the congregation, children with autism can be brought into the church family. "Ask and you shall receive." Ministering to the less fortunate should be one of the core functions of the church. In biblical times, one can imagine people with autism being described as possessed by evil spirits. Jesus walked and lived among these people, performing miracles by casting out their demons. Shouldn't modern-day Christians also aspire to this ideal?

WHAT GRANDPARENTS CAN DO

Grandparents should be supportive, not directive, and certainly not critical of their children and grandchildren. Parents are in the best position to know the capabilities of their child with autism. Grandparent support could be in the form of transportation to church and picking the child up after education sessions. Depending on the child's and parents' wishes, a pizza, burger, or ice cream treat on the way home from religion classes may be appropriate.

Ask your grandchild how classes are going. Show interest that says, "I care about how you are doing in your classes." This applies to any activity in which a child is involved. If they talk on the telephone, it is sometimes easier to get a response by phone than face-to-face because of distractions when together.

Go with the family to church if distance makes this practical. Retreat into the narthex with your grandchild if crowds or music overwhelm him, giving an opportunity for parents to have a meaningful worship experience.

If prayer is part of your personal spiritual life, add intercessory prayer for your grandchild and his family.

If it is part of your spiritual life, witness by showing the importance of faith and worship in your own life, thus showing the child with autism that it is not just his parents who attend church services.

When appropriate, ask questions that may lead to a discussion concerning the developing child's beliefs.

Read Bible stories or other stories that are faith-based to your grandchild, always with the approval of their parents and with the realization that the child with autism may not tolerate stories being read to him or her.

Empathize with other children in the family if the antics of an autistic sibling or cousin are causing embarrassing situations. Sometimes a chat with Grandma or Grandpa can vent their frustrations with the worship situation.

PREPARING FOR EMPLOYMENT

Micah Gets a Job

When Micah was nearing his sixteenth birthday, my husband Hollis and I were discussing his situation, as we often do. "It will not be long until he reaches the end of his high school days. What is in store for him then? Will he attend a college or trade school? Or will there be a willing employer, one with the patience and experience to employ a person with autism?"

By the time they are sixteen, most young people have experiences which have honed working skills or alerted them to the facets of working at a job. Micah was not in that group. His relative immaturity and withdrawal from social encounters left him naïve and unprepared for the working world.

As we contemplated what could be done for Micah, we concluded we had a small learning opportunity for him right in our house. We were in the midst of moving into a new home. Micah and his family would be helping us with the move. This occasion was excellent for giving Micah practice at taking instructions from someone other than parents and doing something more than his usual household chores. Working for Grandma and Grandpa was not like a "real job," but we thought we could give some training for his eventual entry into the working world.

This idea was cleared with Micah's mother and father, and later we placed a call to their home. As we expected, the phone was answered by Micah. After the usual routine salutations, Hollis said, "We want to hire you to help us move into our new home."

Without expressing excitement or reluctance, or inquiring about what would be expected of him, Micah agreed, "Well, O.K.," consenting as we knew he would. Arrangements were made for Stuart and him to come to our new home the next day to help with the move.

To help make this occasion into a real job atmosphere, we decided Micah should complete a time sheet. As Micah came into the house, immediately Hollis said, "Let's get started! We will pay you five dollars an hour. Here is a paper called a time sheet. Write down the time you start in this column. The time you stop in this column. The total time you work in this column."

Micah wrote the starting time. Hollis told him, "Now, please go into the garage. It is full of empty boxes, stacked high, from the move. Here is a knife, but be very careful with it. Use the knife to cut the tape holding the boxes together and flatten the boxes onto the garage floor."

Over an hour went by, and Hollis decided he better check how the project was progressing. He found Micah had flattened all the boxes, but had left them scattered over the entire floor. He had put the knife away and was pacing back and forth in the garage, chattering to himself, skipping and hopping about. Hollis had assumed Micah would stack the flattened boxes and come into the house for another assignment. He then realized he should have given detailed and complete instructions. "You can stack the boxes in this corner and then come into the house, Micah."

He did so, then silently stood in the hallway until Hollis said, "Now, please go downstairs and carry the empty boxes from there up into the garage and flatten them." Since most of the boxes were so large, only one could be carried at a time. This would require numerous trips up and down sixteen stair steps. Hollis relished assigning this task to someone with younger legs, for he had already made many trips up and down the stairs, bringing boxes up to the garage.

Later, when Hollis checked on Micah's progress, he was chagrined but proud of Micah's ingenuity. Instead of following Grandpa's instructions to carry the boxes to the garage and then flatten them, Micah on his own had decided to flatten the boxes downstairs before carrying them to the garage. Thus, he could carry several boxes each trip. He was saving numerous trips up the stairs because he had chosen to do the task his way, differently than Grandpa had instructed.

It was not long before we heard sounds from another part of the house. It was Micah running back and forth, making unusual noises. We were accustomed to and accepting of this behavior, but because we were creating a job atmosphere, we were compelled to stop him. Hollis called out, "Hey Micah, now that you are through with the boxes, come and help me assemble these two sets of shelves. We will take all of the pieces out of the box, and check this list called a bill of material to see if all of the parts are there. Then you can hold the parts together while I put the screws in place! I won't tighten them until we have all of the pieces together and properly lined up."

While Grandpa watched, Micah slowly and deliberately checked the parts, making an X next to each part on the list as he found them, and then they started the shelf assembly.

"Now that we have this first shelf together, you can tighten the screws while I go and help Grandma with what she is doing." When Hollis returned, he found Micah had not only tightened the screws, but on his own had started the assembly of the second set of shelves. Pleasantly surprised, Hollis said, "Nice work, Micah. Finish assembling the shelves, and when you are through I will help you carry them into the closet where they belong."

I was pleased how new shelves made the closet more useful, but more pleased that Micah took the initiative to successfully assemble the second shelf. Micah rarely expresses his feelings, but he seemed to be pleased with his work as he helped me bring items into the closet. "Good job, Micah! The shelves are beautiful."

"Ya," was the response, but without feeling or looking into my eyes.

There was a large carpet downstairs that needed to be carried out of the house. Hollis called, "Hey Stu, please help me carry that heavy rolled-up carpet from downstairs out to your truck. It is a heavy bugger." Hollis was a little anxious about this task. Not concerned for his six-foot-four, two-hundred-thirty-pound son, but for himself, at age eighty, near the end of a physically challenging day, carrying that heavy load up a long flight of stairs.

Upon surveying the situation, Stuart called out, "Micah, come help me carry this carpet." Hollis was caught short. He assumed Micah was not capable of that kind of work. At six-foot-three-inches tall, Micah's string bean physique was rapidly developing, but he did not appear strong enough to lug a heavy, unwieldy carpet. Grandpa said nothing; of course he respected Stuart's judgment. He planned to let them carry the load to the stairs and then get between them to help carry the heavy rug up the stairs. As it turned out, there was no room for him, and he had to simply watch as his son and grandson successfully struggled to get up the stairs.

At the end of the day, Micah completed the time sheet. With Grandpa's help, they calculated Micah's wage. Because of his proven math skills in high school, we believed Micah was capable of making the calculations himself, but he could not be motivated to do so. At the end of a long day, Hollis decided not to force the issue. "Thank you, Micah; you were a big help today. Let me shake your hand, and I will get the money you earned."

Micah showed no emotion when given his wage, just a "Thank you." Was there a slight curl to his mouth? The beginning of a smile? Did he feel some satisfaction with his work? We hoped he did. Grandpa had a new appreciation for Micah's abilities but also remaining anxieties about his future.

DISCUSSION

As grandparents, we naturally concern ourselves about our grandchildren and their future. When the child has autism, the concern leads to anxiety due to all of the unknowns we face. Historical data are not encouraging.

Only six percent of people with autism spectrum disorders have full-time employment according to the National Autism Society, as reported in 2006. This discouraging statistic is reflective of the training and therapy given in past years. Certainly programs available to young people today should result in an increase in opportunities for employment. The extensive education and direction Micah and young people his age receive gives us hope for his ability to work productively one day.

Micah has benefited from some wonderful programs which have been available only in recent years. By 1970 there was some understanding of the autistic mind, but until 1980 little was being done to educate people with autism. Most were institutionalized, as was the character portrayed by Dustin Hoffman in the movie, *Rain Man*. About twenty-five years ago, professionals working with autistic persons decided their improvement would be greater if they remained with their families and most were mainstreamed into public schools at an early age.

Since Micah has been involved with special programs, public education, therapies, and a stable home environment, we hope he may have greater opportunity than some adults of previous generations to find employment. Yet we realize training and therapy do not necessarily resolve the problems Micah will encounter in employment. On several occasions, we have puzzled as we listened to young autistic adults with excellent educational credentials tell how they found employment, but were unable to satisfy workplace requirements.

A major deterrent to their success can be attention deficit disorder, which is common among people with autism. Workers become distracted and do not concentrate on the task, thus failing to complete work well within their capabilities. Keeping Micah focused can be a challenge. He can be diverted, as witnessed when we found him in the garage running around and making noises, when he was supposed to be working.

Another obstacle to continuing employment may be reluctance to work with others—a common characteristic of autism, even when working at tasks which require only their personal input. The autistic worker may find it difficult to fit their completion schedules and procedures into compliance with other workers and company expectations. In her writings, author Temple Grandin explains how she faced this problem.

Temple Grandin, an adult spokesperson with autism, has addressed the importance of family life for children. In a book she wrote with Kate Duffy, *Developing Talents,* she advocates entrepreneurship. Self-employment may present an opportunity to work under circumstances which circumvent some typical autistic sensory issues and offer isolation from distracting office hustle, interruptions, imposing schedules, and routines. In their book, Grandin and Duffy cite that fourteen percent of disabled workers are self-employed, whereas eight percent of the general work force are self-employed. This book discusses careers for individuals with Asperger Syndrome and High Functioning Autism.

Another worthy publication is *Autism Advocate* by the Autism Society of America. Volume 46, entitled "Off to Work," helps readers understand the scope of the employment challenge. Periodically, Micah will talk about going to work. Unlike most boys his age, he has little interest in money, although his interest is developing as he realizes he needs money to purchase DVDs and Transformers toys. Micah's motivation for "getting a job" may be that he sees it as a ritual for growing up.

As I watch him rapidly approaching manhood, I think of ways he might be employed, trying to be realistic about his limitations, but cautious not to assume him incapable. I recall a visit we made to a large sawmill in Montana when Micah was thirteen. It was a fun adventure watching giant logs tumble from the huge trucks into the screaming saws, banging conveyors, and other noisy machinery. Boards of all sizes zoomed from one work station to the other, unguided by human hands. The rapid transition from logs into beautifully stacked, exactly dimensioned boards was amazing. But I was ever fearful that the noise, dust, and high-energy motion would terrify Micah. Micah's response as we left the mill was "I could work there."

The sawmill experience encourages me to be cautious of assuming Micah will not be capable of finding meaningful work. Perhaps it was an indication that Micah can overcome his limitations with exposure to environments he likes. I surmise he was fascinated by the machinery and intrigued by the small, compact containments where operators' computers controlled the robots, and he became oblivious to the noise. Micah is fond of machinery, loves computers, and enjoys compact confines. Being comfortable in compact surroundings is common among those on the autism spectrum. That Micah did not experience his usual aversion to noisy conditions is similar to his acceptance of noise in bowling alleys, movie theaters, and airplanes—places where he tolerates noise because he loves being there.

Since Micah is not heavily motivated by money and finds it difficult to do something which has little interest to him, finding something within his scope of interests is essential. Thus developing his interests towards attainable situations is paramount. Micah's seventeen-year-old-friend Riley, who is also on the spectrum, has had such an experience. At age fifteen or sixteen, Riley's mother put him to work taking care of the horses and doing barn chores where Riley and Micah take riding lessons with the Special Olympics Equestrian Team. Riley has developed into a very energetic and skillful worker with horses and people. Working with horses definitely holds a future for Riley. We were thrilled when recently Riley's mother volunteered to put Micah to work in the barn as a volunteer.

The results were amazing! Micah eagerly accepted the challenge. He showed little trepidation when brushing horses, going into their stalls to put on a halter. He picked up the horses hooves and scraped them, nudging their thousand-pound bodies to a new position, and talking to them as he worked. Cleaning manure and feeding horses was fun for Micah. Mary Lou, Riley's mom, has been a great help to Micah. She understands horses and kids, and is dedicated to helping young people.

Micah's parents have another developmental program underway. He is now in the egg business. He feeds chickens, gathers, cleans, and boxes eggs, and sells them to friends and relatives. He establishes the selling price by visiting the grocery store and collects money from his customers. This is an excellent program for developing the entrepreneur as suggested by Grandin and Duffy.

Reflecting on our hiring Micah, I believe most employers could be satisfied with Micah's work pace—not speedy, but steady. The time he took to knock down the boxes was good, but an employer might expect the boxes to be neatly stacked instead of scattered about the floor. Hollis assumed some sort of gathering of boxes to be part of the task, but did not tell Micah. Perhaps this shortcoming is a characteristic of a young boy's performance, not of an autistic performance. However, I do think it is expected for even a young boy to come out of the garage when finished, instead of just pacing and running. Micah's assembling of the second shelves without being told and breaking down the boxes before carrying them upstairs were excellent indicators that he can be productive on his own.

His going off and running about the house is another matter. This failure to stick with the job would be difficult for an employer to accept. Now, it might be accepted as another young boy characteristic, but failure to concentrate on the task was a problem common to the speakers who told us about their difficulties in keeping their jobs.

The carpet-carrying task was a good lesson for us. When Hollis assumed Micah could not carry the carpet he denied Micah an opportunity to develop his capabilities. Protecting our loved ones is natural, but overprotection can be unkind and limiting. Micah is not as capable as other teens, but we must keep him challenged and not underestimate his abilities.

Some bumps in our hiring Micah were caused by communication difficulty, which is common with those on the autism spectrum. It may be necessary for the employer to be trained in the thinking process of the worker. Some autism societies, regional and state, are now sponsoring workshops for employers who care to learn how to successfully employ young people on the spectrum.

Even though I have spent much time with Micah, I still need to concentrate on how I communicate. For example, it would be natural for me to say, "Micah, would you like to take out the garbage?" In my mind I am telling him in a nice way to do something. Now, I realize his literal mind might interpret my question as my wanting to know if he likes carrying garbage, and naturally he thinks he would rather be watching television. Being openly honest, he might respond with a "No," whereas he is perfectly willing to do the chore. Now I realize saying, "Micah, please carry out the garbage now," works well with him and gets the job done.

If asked to make a choice between two or more of his favorite activities, he will likely respond, "I do not know," Whereas, to start him thinking about his choices by saying things like, "I imagine the car show will have lots of convertibles," or "It would be fun to eat pizza at the bowling alley," will likely result in a definite choice.

For some time, Micah's parents have involved him in work projects, including cooking, house maintenance, and gardening. Micah appears to particularly enjoy working with his father while using tools. For a while we thought Micah might be destined to be a plumber. At about age six, Micah watched as his dad worked on a toilet in their house. Not long after, they learned of an incident in Micah's classroom. They found Micah had used the toilet adjacent to the classroom. Shortly after he returned, the teacher was shocked as water came flowing into the room. Micah had decided to do as he had seen his father do—take the lid off the water closet. He dropped it, breaking the ceramic water closet.

Again one day, Stuart was fixing a faucet in the bathroom sink at home. He had shut off the water supply valve, taken off the faucet, and headed for the hardware store. Micah, the six-year-old plumber, doing as his father had done, decided to open the shut-off valve. Water gushed from the missing faucet connection, flooding a large area. Lesson learned: Take Micah with you when working on a project. He has an inquisitive mind.

In her book, *Understanding the Nature of Autism*, Janice E. Janzen concludes, "While those with autism present major challenges, they also provide major rewards for anyone who takes the opportunity to understand their unique perspective."

Micah's grandfather and I have found rewards.

WHAT GRANDPARENTS CAN DO

Job coaches can assist in securing successful employment. The required qualifications of a coach will vary widely, depending on the ability of the student and demands of the job. They may simply monitor routine activities such as filling out time sheets or arriving at the correct work station. In some situations, a grandparent may feel comfortable performing as coach or sharing responsibility with someone else. Assisting with expenses involved is another possibility.

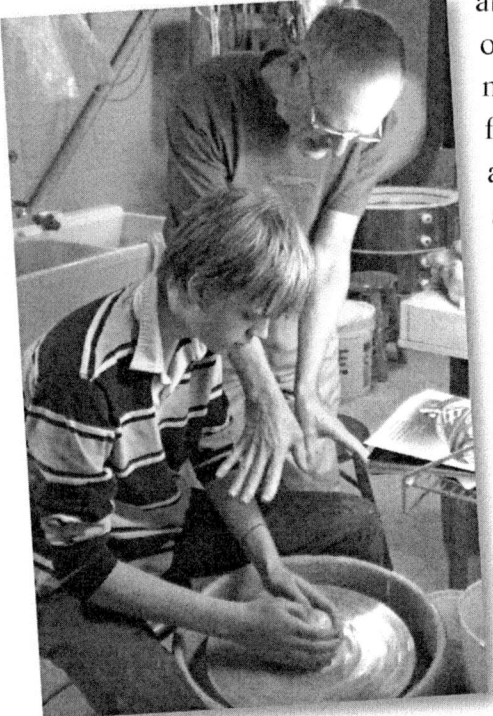

Grandpa Baxter and Micah at the pottery wheel.

Employment opportunities often come through personal contacts. Temple Grandin's first job was sewing for a neighbor. Grandparents can be aware of possible job opportunities among friends and longtime associates.

Micah's maternal grandparents, Jane and Harlan Baxter, have been influential in developing life interests and skills with Micah.

They have engaged him in fishing and bird watching. His Grandpa Baxter has taught him how to make pottery, a skill Micah also enjoys at his high school.

Children develop work skills by observing or participating in activities. Grandparents can help in their development during a child's visits to their home. Activities such as baking, household maintenance, or manual arts hobbies could be vehicles of learning. From early on, grandparents can join the team needed for preparing a young adult for the time he seeks employment.

FINANCIAL FUTURE

Setting Up a Special Needs Trust

Grandparents need to be aware of the financial consequences of giving money or an inheritance to their grandchildren with autism. Both parents and grandparents should become familiar with a Special Needs Trust, a vehicle for the support of an autistic adult without causing loss of legislative entitlements. If a child or adult inherits or is given funds directly, not through a trust, he or she may lose eligibility for government entitlements now or in the future. Entitlements are limited to autistic adults with minimal assets. Funds in a Special Needs Trust may be withdrawn by a trustee for the benefit of the child or adult, but are not counted as assets.

The autism society branch in the area where a child resides should have names of attorneys qualified in Special Needs Trusts. Grandparents can be helpful seeking out details in setting up such a trust.

A Closing Thought

Hollis and I revel in watching our five grandchildren reach adulthood. They brighten our aging lives in numerous ways. When we are with them, we experience the vitality of their youth.

We enjoy the exciting world of collegiate football through Taylor and Connor, who play on university teams. With Muriel we have long experienced the wonderful world of vocal music, which she continues to pursue in college. Hannah's engagement with tennis from junior high into high school has been fun to follow. All four will lead productive lives.

Of the five, it is Micah who may give us the greatest purpose for living in future years. We are thrilled by each step he takes to come out of the world of autism and into the realm of a meaningful life.

To Micah From Grandpa

There are times when I stop and wonder
  What that world of yours has to offer
  An attraction so dominant and strong
    You choose that place to belong

  It's quite tempting I must confess
    To join you there if I could
An easier world for you and me, I guess
But we can't do that for your own good.

Hollis Grubb

Acknowledgments

My greatest appreciation goes to my husband, Hollis Grubb. He encouraged and inspired me, and supplied information and edited for many hours.

I am also grateful for the assistance of the following groups: the Saddlebrooke Writers, the Scribblers of Stillwater, and Meg Park's Pima College classes.

I also want to acknowledge the helpfulness to our family and to Micah over the years from Dennis Moser, Mary Williams, Jackie Patrick, Lynn Foster, Corrine LaGrave, Allison McGuiness, Mary Lou Fiala, and Neil Spofford. Other groups played a major role in Micah's life and were an inspiration to my writing: the faculty of Stillwater Public Schools, staff at Trinity Lutheran Church in Stillwater, staff at St. Croix Courage Center, River Valley Riders, and Special Olympics.

Bibliography

BOOKS

Ariel, Cindy N. and Robert Naseff, ed. *Voices from the Spectrum: Parents, Grandparents, Siblings, People with Autism and Professionals Share Wisdom* (London and Philadelphia: Jessica Kingsley Publications, 2006).

Grandin, Temple and Kate Duffy. *Developing Talents: Careers for Individuals with Asperger Syndrome and High-Functioning Autism* (Shawnee Mission, Kansas: Autism Asperger Publishing, 2004).

Temple Grandin has autism and is a frequent lecturer on the subject. She is an animal scientist who designs livestock-handling facilities worldwide and is a professor of animal sciences at Colorado State University. Her other publications include *Emergence: Labeled Autistic* and *Thinking in Pictures*.

Janzen, Janice E., M.S. *Understanding the Nature of Autism* (San Antonio: Therapy Skill Builders, 1996).

Notbohm, Ellen, and Veronica Zysk. *1001 Great Ideas for Teaching and Raising Children with Autism Spectrum Disorders* (Arlington, Texas: Future Horizons, 2004).

Sicile-Kira, Chantal. *Adolescents on the Spectrum* (New York: Berkley/Penguin, 2006).

Siegel, Bryna. *The World of the Autistic Child, Understanding and Treating Autism Spectrum Disorders* (New York: Oxford University Press, 1996).

Wolfburg, Pamela J. *Play and Imagination in Children with Autism* (New York: Columbia University, 1999).

ORGANIZATIONS

Key additional resources on autism are the Autism Society of America and the autism societies of individual states.

WEBSITES

Among the many helpful websites offering information on autism are:

Autism Speaks (www.autismspeaks.org), sponsored by Bob and Suzanne Wright, which has become a global resource on autism.

Autism Society of America (www.autismsociety.org).

Autism Spectrum Quarterly (www.ASQuarterly.com).